Love
in the
House

Love in the House

Filling your home with the Greatest Commandment

ISBN: 978-0-9795642-0-8

Printed in the United States of America
Monument Publishing, Colorado

To our children:

Alicia, Alissa, Cynthia, Lydia, Isaiah, Micah, Noah, Tabitha, Keilah, Hannah, Josiah, Havilah, Joshua, and our baby due to be born later in 2007

And to our grandson,

Isaak

Table of Contents

About the Cover

The cover art was drawn by 14-year-old Morgan Adams, the oldest of nine Adams children. Morgan has a special artistic talent. She has authored, with her mother, several children's books. One book, *Arrows in His Hands,* was written for the Jeub family at the birth of their twins in 2005. The Adams family has been friends with the Jeubs for several years.

Acknowledgements

Love in the House is a book about family. There were many family members who helped polish the message on love that we have here in this book. Alicia was a major player in maturing the message of love and strengthening our family. My (Chris's) mother, Judy, has been a prayer warrior for me throughout my life, and her prayers are felt every day. My (Wendy's) sisters Heather, Paula and Debbi are witnesses of familial love that is most appreciated.

We have many good friends to thank, too. Jeff, the best copy-editor we know, thanks for your blunt disagreements and sharpening of our message. Karen Hamer (mother of seven), Robin Douglas (mother of eight), Nancy Erickson (mother of four), and Donita Fueshko (mother of seven), thank you for taking time from your busy schedules to help fine-tune our message. Eric Ludy, friend and partner in ministry, thank you for pointing us in the right direction.

We have received love from our small church fellowship, and they have been integral players in the articulation of this powerful mission. Each family walks in faith and love of Jesus Christ and proves it by loving God and loving us. We could not have labored through writing this book without walking through lessons on love together.

Foreword

By John Fuller

I have *only* six children. I'm pretty sure that before we decided to marry, my wife and I talked about having just four kids. Our first was born in 1988, and it was a joyous occasion. Over the next 10 years we were blessed with four more children. And then, with the sense that God was (rather inexplicably at the time) leading us to expand our family once more, we adopted an infant from Russia. Adding that little bundle made six. How did we end up with six kids? I thought we agreed to four...

Each of our children is a uniquely wonderful gift to our lives, and Dena and I have grown accustomed to the blessings that come with them. We're now quite used to the cute comments, little jokes, or probing questions as people notice that we have more children than "average." "Don't you know what causes that?" some have asked with wry grins. We have been judged as being especially religious, following some church prescription against birth control. Or perhaps we've had an "accident" or two? Accident or not, we are grateful for each outcome.

We're used to the chaos that a large family sometimes (*always?*) brings. The children have the normal range of interests, friends, and activities. So we drive them around a lot, we balance schedules and the overall needs of the family, and we often live at a fast pace. I cannot imagine being busier, nor can I imagine a more fulfilling life.

We're used to the expenses of a large family, too. My two oldest sons are taller than me, and as teen boys are prone to do, *they eat*. And eat. And eat. They seem to outgrow their clothing before seasons change, and the younger kids are following suit! We drive three gas-guzzlers: a van, an SUV and a nine-passenger Suburban. Together they average how many miles-per-gallon…? Oh, never mind. It doesn't matter, really, because we need the room to haul our precious cargo of kids.

Most people would say I have a lot of kids, but I have less than *half* the number of children as Chris and Wendy Jeub! In a culture that elevates convenience and personal goals over higher ideals such as sacrifice and selflessness, this unique family really stands out. They can't go anywhere without drawing some stares. I know they don't seek attention, but it is inevitable to stop and pause when you see Mrs. Jeub at the store followed by—how many are there?—six, eight or ten kids? The Jeubs experience a lot of inquisitive looks, unsolicited comments and unusual questions as they go about their daily lives, but they welcome the curiosity. They've had to think through the commitments and responsibilities of parenting more than a dozen children, and the pages of *Love in the House* are filled with many of these thoughts.

I've gotten to watch the Jeub family grow over the years. Chris and I worked together at Focus on the Family before he left to put more time into a ministry devoted to home school teens, in which my sons participate with Chris as their academic debate coach. Chris and Wendy have welcomed the arrival of each newborn child with faith that God will provide for their needs. Their testimony proves that He always does! The Jeubs wrestle with the same challenges that most parents have to face, but they have a remarkable fearlessness about having so many children and the corresponding responsibilities. I know their story will encourage you in your own parenting.

In the following pages you'll enjoy practical examples of how the Jeubs manage a family of 15—and some pretty unusual stories as well. But at the heart of this book you'll see a deep, profound love for children as gifts from the Lord. It is this *love* that is a timeless example every family can learn from. The Jeubs have lived out that timeless attitude with great effect upon me, and now, upon you.

John Fuller is vice president of Focus on the Family's Audio and New Media division. He has been the co-host of the daily "Focus on the Family" radio program, joining Dr. James C. Dobson in the studio for the broadcast, which reaches millions of global listeners each week.

Introduction

This book was born out of our experience with TLC (formerly The Learning Channel) and Powderhouse Productions—a TV production company that contracted with TLC—when we were one of three families featured in the miniseries "Kids by the Dozen." Powderhouse contacted us in the spring of 2006 to see if we were interested in doing the show. A producer asked us if there were any big events coming up, and we gave them a few ideas. Our annual Jeub Birthday Bash, a once-a-year party we throw for all our kids, was the idea that Powderhouse latched on to. It was agreed: they would come out and follow us for eight days leading up to the party.

The onsite producer came out to see us before taping began. A single man, he took to our children almost immediately and was soon behaving more like an uncle to them than a producer. Moreover, he had been around reality television since the genre started. "Reality," he told us, "is what people genuinely want to know, and we want to know what a family of 15 does to get by." They want to know how we do all that laundry and wash all those dishes, how we educate the kids, how we can afford to take care of so many. To his credit, the producer seemed genuinely interested in capturing on camera the reality of daily life for a family of 15.

The crew consisted of a cameraman, a sound guy, and the associate producer and onsite producer. They stayed at a nearby bed-and-breakfast, showed up at scheduled times and followed us throughout the days. Much of the coverage ended up on the editing floor. Home school, work, the birthday party, the story of our daughter Alicia, and shopping as a family all made it into the finished product. Some schooling activities, Wendy's women's group, Sunday morning church, and several hours of interviews were all cut. Over 50 hours of footage were captured through the week, all of which was edited down to a 44-minute episode that was broadcast on TLC in January 2007.

The producer advised us early on that this would be an experience unlike any other. We looked into the camera for many, many hours, explaining why we live the way we live, why we have so many children, and how we make it all work. We talked of our faith and our values. We ended up enjoying the opportunity because we grew through it immensely.

As the week progressed, the crew captured preparations for the party, schooling, shopping, work and so on. We opened up about our estranged relationship we had with our oldest daughter, Alicia, and how her contact with the family was extremely limited. The producer didn't want to pry, but told us up front that this might be a compelling angle for the episode, as long as Alicia was up for it. We were honest with him: We were separated from our daughter because of a long history of failures and frustrations, but we all desired reconciliation. The producer went back to New York and pitched the idea to the network executives. He returned a month later and captured much of what was presented on the show. The final chapters of this book go into detail about what was not shown on television.

The experience was unlike any other, since it spurred us to reflect on our way of life, and eventually to write this book. There were a number of themes that surfaced throughout the week, and these six themes are spread throughout the 12 chapters you're about to read. We can't tell you how much feedback we've gotten since the show first aired, but we will do our best to address the questions most people have about our family philosophy. Here, in a nutshell, are those six themes:

1. Fear

We'd love to say that we live fearless lives, but that would be untrue. We all have fears that keep us from moving in the direction that God wants us to move. Especially when considering the blessing of children, fears—though they may be unfounded—play a big role in our decision making. We spend a considerable amount of time identifying the most common fears and addressing them. Indeed, we hear from many young couples who fear (like we did in the past) the idea of bringing children into the world. Chapters 1 and 2 represent our attempt to help couples face—and overcome—those fears.

2. Creativity

We posted a survey on our website (*www.jeubfamily.com*) the night our "Kids by the Dozen" episode first aired, asking what people liked most about the show. Overwhelmingly, people chose Shopping/Saving Money. For those people, Chapters 3 and 4 will be interesting chapters, since they answer many of the questions people have about our family finances. We manage fine on an income of less than $40,000 per year, so creative spending is definitely important. We'll share some examples of how we provide for such a large family on a small income, and we'll also try to help you do the same by tapping into your God-given creative juices.

3. Freedom

Some critics of our lifestyle would argue that we are enslaved to our children. We couldn't disagree more. We'll explain in the chapters on freedom how a life with many children is an incredibly liberating life. We believe the notion of children as bondage is a rather recent concept. In fact, throughout history, large families were seen as more of a blessing than a hindrance. This can be attributed to a modern cultural attitude toward family and children, but we'll also explore some of the pitfalls that parents bring upon themselves.

4. Child Rearing

We have a new saying we like to tell parents: Parent as if there is a camera crew following you around every day. In preparation for the taping, we sharpened our parenting as much as possible. We aren't perfect parents, but knowing that the cameras were coming, we prepared ahead of time. Much of the feedback we received after the show aired was from parents who wanted to know how we raise our children. Frustrated moms from chaotic homes wrote us and begged for our "secrets." We'll share what we've learned over the years, but the truth is that there aren't any secrets, just tried and true methods for reestablishing order in the household.

5. Relationships

While we have received an overwhelming amount of positive feedback, we have nonetheless received a handful of "hate mail," primarily from people who are appalled by how we shelter our children from the real world. "Get those kids in school!" one person wrote. "It is irresponsible to bring more kids into the world when you live in poverty." "How can you be drinking all that Starbucks while you let your kids go without socks?" (Yes, we drank a lot of Starbucks coffee the week of the show, but that was only because the producer brought it to the house every morning. And, of course, our kids do wear socks.)

We'll demonstrate how a large family carries with it some natural socializing factors. In fact, some recent studies have shown that parents aren't necessarily the primary influencers of their children's character. In many cases, siblings play a larger role. As you'll see, a family of 13 kids is definitely a social environment worth studying.

6. Love

The most challenging part of the book to write—and perhaps for you to read—deals with our oldest daughter, Alicia. The TLC episode accurately portrayed our estranged relationship with Alicia, but there was much more to the story—a lot more than would fit neatly into a 44-minute show. We are thankful for how everything turned out, especially because Alicia is now reunited with the family. Along the way, we all learned a lesson in love that we'll attempt to articulate in the final chapters. The lesson is what our family is all about: our lives, our faith, and our mission in life.

Our mission in life is why we wrote this book. We believe we're onto something here. Like most parents, we're doing the best we can as life goes on, but our feeble steps of faith have produced some insights that we want to share with you. We make our lives transparent because we believe families and couples would appreciate learning more about parenting and the value of children. This book is not our attempt to show how perfect we are; quite the contrary, this book unveils some of our deepest faults and struggles. What we learned along our journey as parents are significant truths that we wished we mastered many years ago. If our vulnerability encourages others to grow healthy, loving families, then this book will have been worth the effort. *Love in the House* is what we are, and this book is a reflection of our love.

Chapter 1

Fears of Having Children

Late one night, the Jeub family was traveling through northern New Mexico on the way home from a visit to Arizona. Our transportation, a converted 1984 GMC school bus, broke down in the desert south of Shiprock. The engine made a large *bang* and went dead. The 18,000-pound tank of steel managed to barely clear a hill, at which point gravity took over. We coasted down the hill and into the parking lot of a Mustang Gas Station. The station was closed, so we rolled up next to a semi truck and parked. It was 1:30 a.m.

Most of the kids were asleep as we popped the hood and tried to determine the problem. The engine would not respond, so we decided to get some rest and call a tow truck in the morning. We were about 600 miles from home, traveling through a Navajo Indian Reservation, a nation within a nation, in the middle of an unfamiliar culture and set of laws.

The next morning, we discovered that our bus had died at the intersection between a factory and several hundred Native American homes. Truck after truck of Navajo men rolled through the gas station, fueled up, grabbed coffee and breakfast, and headed to the factory. We brought our blonde-haired children (11 at the time) into the gas station to warm up and eat breakfast. The local residents couldn't have been friendlier. The cashiers—though busy—made sure we had the information we needed for towing services. Gruff-looking factory workers smiled at us as they made their way through the store. An elderly woman—perhaps in her 80s—asked Wendy if all these children were hers. "You are a blessed woman!" she said with a smile. We realized that our anxieties about being stranded in the middle of an Indian reservation were based on our fear of the unknown and personal prejudice. We were strangers in a strange land, but our concerns were largely unfounded.

An oversized tow truck arrived within a couple of hours, and our entire family squeezed into the back for the 30-mile trip to the repair shop.

We phoned a friend from our church in Colorado to let him know of our predicament. After telling him where we were, he said, "I think there was someone who visited the church yesterday from that area!" A few phone calls later, we connected with a local family who offered us a warm meal and a place to stay for the night. We ate heartily and enjoyed rich conversation while the bus was repaired. We set off early the next morning with freshly baked cookies for the ride home and new friendships to ponder.

We'd been stranded in the desert, in the midst of a "foreign nation," traveling with 11 children all under 13 years old, but we had little reason to fear. Reflecting back on the entire situation, we saw that God had taken care of us every step of the way. The Mustang Gas Station was seemingly in the middle of nowhere, yet we managed to coast into the parking lot. The intersection was packed with friendly people who helped us in our time of need. And our home church—some 600 miles away—had *the day before* welcomed visitors who lived just a few miles from the repair shop. The mechanic, too, was a gift—our bus has been running great ever since.

For many parents, traveling with children is a highly stressful experience. They worry about the unexpected, that they will be stranded without any help or, worse yet, in real danger. Add children to an anxious situation and with it comes an incredible burden of responsibility. Our experience in New Mexico is one of many experiences where God's hand was in all our adventure—especially during the anxious moments.

Many people suffer from a fear of abandonment, yet our faith reminds us to pray for "our daily bread"—our basic needs—and trust God to provide. God calmed our fears by providing our needs. Yet the fear of being unable to provide—or the fear that God won't do so—leads many to limit their family size. Though they know in theory to trust God for "our daily bread," in reality they do not. We read in Scripture that children are blessings from God, yet we often fall short of believing that God will provide the means to feed, clothe and house these blessings. The media reinforces the notion nowadays that having children—let alone raising them—is a daunting prospect. Indeed, we have also faced this fear, but we are living proof that it is without merit, *especially* in our world today. The rest of this chapter will build the case that parents today are in the *best* cultural situation to bear and raise children.

Parenthood: What Are We Afraid Of?

Many new parents—as well as childless couples contemplating a life of parenthood—share some common fears that we have likewise struggled with. Many of these fears are addressed in this book with remedies and anecdotes we have (often out of sheer necessity) discovered or created ourselves. We believe children are blessings from God, but we're not "super parents." We've struggled with the same fears that many soon-to-be parents face, but we are here to testify that those fears are largely false. Now, let's look at some of the common fears young couples have about raising children.

Fear of Rejection

The life Wendy and I live—raising 13 children and willing to have more—is seen by many as a bit crazy. Families who have more than, say, three children are considered "large." Such families aren't typically invited over to others' homes (how could they feed all of them?).

Some people have called us irresponsible, even reckless, for having so many children. Thankfully, our own parents support our way of life, but we know of many like-minded couples who have been scorned by members of their own family.

Be prepared: If you choose to have more than three children, you, too, will likely be subject to wisecracks. Don't listen to them; listen instead to like-minded parents. Whether they've raised one child or 10, most parents will never say their children were not a blessing to them. Why pay attention to folks who don't know any better? Once children come into your life, you'll see the miraculous blessing they are, and all those worries about how your neighbor/sibling/co-worker/whomever might view you will simply vanish.[1]

Fear of Lost Opportunities

It is easy to fall victim to this one. Ask someone to describe the "glamorous life," and it would probably involve travel, fame, achievements, wealth and the like. Now, we're the first to admit that our life with 13 children isn't exactly "glamorous." We live in a modest home; I (Wendy) spend most of my days not going anywhere; and I (Chris) work long hours trying to make ends meet. We've never traveled outside North America, and we barely make it outside Colorado. We're not even close to famous—the TLC experience notwithstanding. This begs the question: Are we somehow missing out on the best that life has to offer?

But how do you weigh the value of children against the values that popular culture deems important? How many parents would trade their children for the riches or opportunities of the childless? It is true that the childless have freedoms most parents don't get to enjoy. Most of the TLC crew (producers, editors, cameramen, etc.) were either single or married with no children. One of the crew recently sent us a postcard from the coasts of Antarctica. We'd love to travel there, but under the circumstances it is basically impossible. Chris' cousin is a single man, and he has countless stories of African safaris and exotic travels around the world. The reality is that having 13 kids keeps us from traveling much at all. Our bus gets five miles to the gallon, and flying our family one time zone away would cost several thousand dollars.

While having a large family has indeed limited some of our travel opportunities, it has opened the door to many other rich adventures we would not have experienced without our children. A few years back, we set a goal as a married couple. I (Chris) would write a bestselling novel that would finance a cross-country trip for the entire family. Needless to say, I am *still* working on that bestselling novel, but we have been blessed beyond our wildest dreams. In 1999 and 2000, when we were only a family of ten, we traveled from coast to coast when our daughter qualified for the national finals of a speech and debate tournament. In 1999, the national tournament was held in Virginia. Along the way, we swam in Lake Erie and the Atlantic Ocean; we toured Washington D.C. and camped in the Appalachian Mountains. The 2000 finals took us to San Diego. We camped in the Black Hills and Yellowstone Park; we swam in the Pacific Ocean and ate in Tijuana, Mexico; we drove through Colorado Springs and visited Focus on the Family. The visit led to a change of career: from public school teacher to journalist.

Did you catch the cause of all these opportunities? It wasn't through much skill of our own. Through our daughter's ability in speech and debate, our dream of cross-country travel was realized.

It is not uncommon for families to build lives around their children's activities. We know a couple with 11 children, Bob and Nina Lawles, whose family activity is music. The Lawles family has traveled across the country singing and performing for churches and community events. Bob and Nina say that, thanks to their children, they've enjoyed many opportunities that they would have never dreamed possible.

What do you enjoy doing with your children? We believe it is good for families to choose activities that everyone—in their own way—can enjoy. For our family, we have embraced academic speech and debate. Our kids compete in tournaments offered through the National Christian Forensics & Communication Association. Your children might prefer sports: The Arndt family, with 14 kids (also featured on TLC's "Kids by the Dozen") host a local softball tournament as a fundraiser for their nonprofit ministry. The other family that appeared on TLC, the Heppners, built their own construction business, the business featured on their episode.

Every family has a chance to *embrace opportunity* as life blesses them with children. This perceived fear of lost opportunity is *simply not real*. Opportunities are still there for large families.

Fear of Lack of Resources

The most common concern among well-meaning people is our family's perceived lack of resources. They worry about our ability to feed so many children, to supply a quality education, to provide adequate shelter, etc. Moreover, there exists a popular mindset that esteems parents who restrict the number of children in a family in order to provide for various materialistic "necessities." In a recent article published in *The Nation* that attempted to explain the large-family movement, a sociologist argued that children today "become a disadvantage, especially to younger kids who don't get as many resources."[2] There is an expectation of failure, this sociologist wrote, among families who are weighed down by children who naturally exhaust their parents and drain the family of its resources.

Will our family reach the point where we are unable to provide for our children? We find that difficult to fathom. Granted, we are anything but wealthy. We water our orange juice down to make it stretch, and we seldom—if ever—buy sirloin steaks from the supermarket. Nearly all our bikes were purchased at garage sales or given to us, and we typically go shopping for clothes just once a year. (We are given used items on a regular basis.) We live in a modest home, we don't have cable television, and our kids do not own the latest video game. Our son Noah once bought an electronic snowboarding game at a garage sale, but it eventually lost its appeal and now serves as a homemade swing hanging from a branch in our backyard!

Some may consider our family poor, but we believe we are *the wealthiest people in the world.* Our kids don't care that they don't have their own bedrooms when right outside the back door is a six-and-a-half acre playground. To them, a "play station" is their latest Lego creation. To our minds, materialism is the shallowest of reasons to shut out the blessing of a large family. We've all read of people who lived in castles yet were filled with sorrow and loneliness. Likewise, don't we all know others who enjoyed rich, satisfying lives, despite their modest means?

One of Chris's best friends growing up was Paul Hanus, the second of 14 children. Paul's parents, Mike and Fran, are devout Catholics who have allowed God to bless them handsomely with children. Mike, however, struggled his entire life with one job layoff after another. They lived on the poor side of town in a run-down, rented house. Their vehicles were in constant need of repair. Yet when Chris visited the Hanus home, the sense of love and loyalty was stronger in that family than among any of his other, wealthier, friends. The Hanuses were the poorest family Chris knew growing up, but they were rich in love and in heavenly blessings.

Our family had the opportunity to visit the Hanus home on a trip to Wisconsin last year. More than 20 years after Chris last saw them, Mike and Fran are down to four kids still living at home. The 10 children now out on their own, meanwhile, have given them a total of, at last count, 29 grandchildren. Much of the family showed up at the house during our visit, and we enjoyed pizza and soda, and reminisced about old times. Mike and Fran served their progeny with pride and joy. Conversation and laughter filled the house, as sons and daughters, sons-in-law and daughters-in-law, grandsons and granddaughters, all got acquainted with the visiting Jeub family.

We saw no evidence that a lack of material resources have kept the Hanus family from enjoying fulfilled lives. Their house is full of love, full of relationships, full of adventure. There was no fear to be found—there wasn't any room.

Fear: The Crippler

There isn't any reason for fears like these to have power in your life. These fears are crippling and, unfortunately, reasons why many young couples choose to restrict the blessing of children. There are some real fears, however. As the next chapter will show, there is a looming threat and a reason why this threat is real.

Chapter 2

A Fear That's Real

We both remember when we feared bearing too many children. Today, that fear is largely a thing of the past. When we talk with other parents of large families, they, for the most part, agree that the most fearful times were when they had less than five children. Parents who allow God to bless them with children on a regular basis often find themselves with five *young* and *needy* children in a relatively short amount of time. That's when fear tries to persuade you to do the "responsible" thing and think about a vasectomy or tubal ligation. Is it too far fetched to suggest that the leading cause of abortions is *fear*? Mothers who fear rejection, lost opportunity, and the inability to provide for their children are many times persuaded that the decision to abort their child is somehow the "responsible" thing to do. We think these fears are false.

We do admit to a serious concern, though it's one that isn't widely publicized. In fact, there are very, very few voices out there talking about it. Now, we don't typically go in for fear mongering. We don't believe the world is melting away, we don't believe we are living in apocalyptic times, and we don't believe using disposable diapers will fill up all the landfills in the world. Some of you may believe these things are true, and you have every right to believe so. However, we are concerned about a much greater threat facing our planet: the threat of *underpopulation.*

You may have laughed just now. Aren't there many more voices in the world warning us about *overpopulation*? Please hear us out. There are a growing number of demographic studies that examine how population aging and decline could be one of the biggest catastrophes of the 21st century. And these warnings come not solely from the right-wing, conservative-Christian, anti-birth-control crowd. One of the most prominent voices is Phillip Longman, a senior fellow at the New America Foundation. His book *The Empty Cradle* examines the incredibly harmful effects of a society that discourages child-bearing. Longman points out a number of facts that, when taken together, paint a disturbing picture:

> Single-child families are prone to extinction. A single child replaces one of his or her parents, but not both. Nor do single-child families contribute much to future population. The 17.4 percent of baby boomer women who had only one child account for a mere 7.8 percent of children born in the next generation. By contrast, nearly a quarter of the children of baby boomers descend from the mere 11 percent of baby boomer women who had four or more children. These circumstances are leading to the emergence of a new society whose members will disproportionately be descended from parents who rejected the social tendencies that once made childlessness and small families the norm.[3]

Using logic and demographic study, Longman makes the argument that a growing population plays a larger role in a civilization's progress than any other factor. To back up his thesis, Longman examines the current population decline in Europe, a decline he suggests will bring about undesirable outcomes.

The dominant media has largely ignored Longman's work—but not completely. The intense and oftentimes militant assault on traditional families in today's political and social environments has a very real and obvious outcome. That's because it isn't money that makes our economy run; it is *people*. As long as a nation's populace remains productive, the society prospers. But in places where reproduction is in decline, the dwindling supply of workers can no longer support the economy. Longman makes the convincing argument that countries like Italy, Germany, France and China—where reproduction is discouraged either through cultural persuasion or government policy—a devastating economic shortfall is inevitable. Just do that math. We have watched the rioting in the streets of Paris, where Islamic youth (the only population still growing in France) have risen up against their aging French neighbors. France has actually taken to paying women to have children, [4] though most women aren't taking the government up on the offer. Every member nation in the European Union has now fallen *below* the birthrate needed to simply sustain the population (meaning less than 2.0 children per couple). This is a threat that should not be ignored.

Fearing Fruitfulness

We find many similarities between Adam and Eve's decision to manipulate their situation with the modern couple's attempt to control their own. The story comes from Chapter 3 of Genesis, where the serpent convinces Eve that death will not result if she eats the forbidden fruit.

> Now the serpent was more crafty than any of the wild animals the Lord God had made. He said to the woman, "Did God really say, 'You must not eat from any tree in the garden'?"

Young couples today are tempted with a variation on this question: "Did God really say, 'Be fruitful and increase in number'?" Did you notice how Satan deceived Eve by focusing on the forbidden rather than the blessing? The entire garden was allowed to Eve, but Satan wanted Eve to focus on the one fruit that was not allowed.

> The woman said to the serpent, "We may eat fruit from the trees in the garden, but God did say, 'You must not eat fruit from the tree that is in the middle of the garden, and you must not touch it, or you will die.'"

The fruitfulness of children is a difficult reflection. Amidst mismatched socks and piling laundry, school activities and homework, limited hot water on Sunday mornings, squabbles and fights, bruises and scraped knees—it is often difficult to reflect on the blessings of children. And when that happens, are we actually being led astray by a fallen cultural persuasion similar to history's first deception?

> "You will not surely die," the serpent said to the woman. "For God knows that when you eat of it your eyes will be opened, and you will be like God, knowing good and evil."

Surely God understands that we can't handle more than a couple kids. Since God has given us the ability to control our reproduction, surely we should do so. Our bodies are fragile, our finances are limited, our mental health can be stretched only so far, our neighbors will think we're nuts, etc., etc., etc.

When we embrace such thinking, we have fallen for the worldly lie that replaces God's plan (be fruitful and increase in number) with our plan ("control" the number of children we have). We don't *die* when we break from God's plan, but our lives are less fruitful. I have yet to meet the parents who willingly followed God's command to be fruitful and multiply only to later regret their decision. Sure, thoughtful parents will reflect on what they could have done differently in raising their many children, but do they ever say, "We wish we had fewer children" or "We wish we weren't blessed with so many kids"? Perhaps we will meet them someday, but we can't imagine finding parents who wish they had never had their children.

Then again, isn't such a twisted, selfish position exactly what is encouraged in our culture? Aren't young couples encouraged today to eat of the fruit of careers, travel and entertainment?

Why allow the fruit of children to interfere with our plans and our will?

> When the woman saw that the fruit of the tree was good for food and pleasing to the eye, and also desirable for gaining wisdom, she took some and ate it. She also gave some to her husband, who was with her, and he ate it. Then the eyes of both of them were opened, and they realized they were naked; so they sewed fig leaves together and made coverings for themselves.

We realize this message is difficult to understand at first. We both have been confronted by those who are quite convinced that restricting the blessing of children is fine—in fact, it's "responsible." We have weighed carefully their reasoning, but we have yet to see how God's Word supports it. We almost laugh at some of their claims because our lives demonstrate the exact opposite!

Take, for example, health. Health is an important consideration when considering something as important as bearing children. Wendy had successfully delivered 11 vaginal births when she got pregnant with our first set of twins. I (Chris) recall sharing with a friend how Wendy's pregnancy was extraordinarily more difficult than the other 11. He quickly admonished me for allowing Wendy to have all these kids: "She's not getting younger, you know!" The assumption in his mind was obvious: Wendy's difficulty in this pregnancy was because she was getting older and her pregnancies were wearing her down. We later found out that Wendy was pregnant with twins, so the reason for the increased difficulty had little (perhaps nothing) to do with Wendy's age, but my friend so quickly assumed this to be the case.

We have found that health—or, more accurately defined, the *fear of unhealthiness*—is a major reason people choose to limit the number of children they have or choose to have no children at all. Many have the notion that pregnancies rob women of physical health. We realize that Wendy is blessed with an extraordinary physical ability to bear children. At 39 years old, she is incredibly healthy even after 13 successful deliveries. However, health concerns could have been used as an excuse to stop having children 10 kids ago! Though health issues trouble even the strongest of people, it seems that the most common excuse given for Wendy's occasional problems—even by medical professionals—is her pregnancies. "It must be because she's been pregnant so many times."

There is a common stereotype of a woman who has had many children. Her body is falling apart—skin and stomach muscles sagging, barefoot, overweight, and careworn as she chases several unkempt and unruly children. *Hardly* the picture of vibrant health and beauty. Perhaps this image is partly responsible for the fear many women harbor about having children. They are afraid of how they may come to look, disappointing to themselves and unattractive to their husbands. In stark contradiction, all three mothers featured on "Kids by the Dozen" were beautiful, thin and radiant. Between the three of them, they gave birth to 43 children.

Depleting health and beauty are only two of the many fears people have that, unfortunately, keep them from procreating. Many couples fear being able to financially provide for their family, and how can parents possibly love all those kids? Stress and anxiety is a fear with only two children; how can the same parents handle four kids? Chaos can be witnessed in a family with only one child; times their one unruly child by 13 and you have a quite a fearsome scenario!

These fears are very practical concerns, which are really fears of the unknown. Most people don't know what it's like to have five, 10, or in our case, 13 children. We remember the fear in our hearts when we, with only five children, considered birth control. We can honestly look back on that fear and recognize how unfounded it really was. We have learned over the years that with every child comes a new blessing and a new adventure. Challenges and trials come with every child, sure, but there has been no trial that has not been overcome.[5] All parents will face struggles, but the fear associated with those struggles may not be so bad. We move forward in faith trusting God to provide whatever resources, financial or emotional, that we may need. Having this faith empowers us to overcome our fears and find the fruitful blessing in God's wonderful admonition to "be fruitful and increase in number."[6]

Chapter 3

Creativity

A common question people ask parents of large families is: "How *do* you do it?" We never have a definitive answer. Sometimes we throw up our arms and admit, "We're making this up as we go along!"

That's what we told the TLC crew that followed us around for eight days. They wanted to capture how life unfolds for a family with 13 kids, yet there is an underlying normality that surprises many observers. Our family is not that different from any other family in this regard: We are making decisions, adapting to life's circumstances and reacting to the trials of this world just like anyone else. We're atypical in how many children we have, but our approach to family and life in general can be applied to families with two kids or twenty.

So, how do we do it? That's what this chapter will attempt to explain. By "it," we mean dealing with those common, frustrating trials that every family faces—only on a larger scale. Few people like to do laundry; how does a family with 13 kids handle it? A budget is tough enough to maintain with a small family nowadays; how do we make ends meet? Dirty dishes often stack up with a family of four; how does a family of 15 manage? Matching socks, trips to the store, driving kids to activities, teaching them to share, preparing meals, making time for a spouse or simply enjoying a moment alone…come to think of it, *how do we do it?*

We do it just like anyone else can: We're creative. Are we more so than most? We don't believe so. God gave us the ability to adapt and adjust, able to make things happen using little but the resources around us. When the need arises, anyone can be innovative and resourceful. The same God who designed couples to create a human being through their love has formed in us the ability to provide for a growing family.

There is a familiar heart-warming line that we've heard from our friends: "I was overwhelmed with the laundry (or schooling or dishes or finances), but I just thought, 'Wendy and Chris are able to do it, why can't I?' So I just kept plugging along with a big smile on my face." We try to live transparent lives because we want to encourage other parents that they *can* do it, too. Modern society tells us that just two kids are a handful. We have been blessed with 13, but we've never faced a challenge that we couldn't overcome.

It may sound corny, but it's true: Attitude is everything. We can talk all day about the tricks and secrets to running a household with 13 kids, but when it comes down to it, all our advice will amount to little if parents have the wrong attitude. The following are attitude changes that we have found are essential in running a household, and they are just as effective whether your family is big or small.

Attitude Change #1: Recognize that God is your ultimate provider.

We must make perfectly clear how incredibly proficient Jesus Christ is in providing us with our "daily bread." We are thoroughly convinced—and evidence pops up all the time in our lives—that God will always provide His children with the necessities of life.

In fact, we'll go out on a limb and say this: It doesn't matter how many kids you have when it comes to meeting your daily needs. God has always kept us at the limits of our finances, but you know what? We have always had enough to pay every bill, we have never gone without food or shelter, and we have never filed for bankruptcy. Even if we had 100 kids, I believe God would still provide for every need.

Yet many parents today embrace the notion that they must be perfectly prepared for the coming of children. Not only should modern parents be mature enough to bear children, they must have all their finances in order before facing the drastic—and expensive—prospect of a baby.

Truth is, they've got it backwards. When it comes to maturity, a young couple can remain forever self-centered and immature if they avoid having children. But once their first baby comes along, that same young couple miraculously starts to mature. They mature out of necessity into the next phase of life: parenthood. Whether through adoption or natural birth, couples who become parents are compelled to *grow up*. We're not saying that people without children are inherently immature.

The couples we're addressing have been married for a few years yet still think children are somewhere (don't know where) in the future. What they don't realize is that the wife has a limited window of opportunity in which to bear children, and if she passes on that opportunity, she (and her spouse) will miss out on the beautiful maturation that comes with raising children.

We have been incredibly blessed to have 13 children, and we hope God will bless us with more. It is important to note, however, that we don't view the blessing of children *quantitatively.* Children are blessings, but we're not necessarily blessed any more than a family with two children. We're not living a competitive life out to have as many children as we can, and we're not encouraging people to do that. What we're living is a life of faith and freedom that opens the heart to receiving the blessing of children. We want to share that freedom with parents; this is at the heart of *Love in the House.* There are too many parents today who believe children are enslaving. Our desire is to counter that belief.

Believe it or not, having children will actually give you a sense of *freedom* that cannot be fully understood until it is experienced. Over the years, we have counseled couples who got it into their minds that bringing children into the world without their college tuition planned for (that's their unborn kids' tuition) is somehow "irresponsible." This kind of thinking will only lead you to delay or even avoid the blessing of children. Put this false logic behind you and trust that God will provide for you and your family. We believe that you will creatively find a way!

Attitude Change #2: Always be adaptable.

Everyone needs a little routine in their lives, but a family with 13 kids also needs to be adaptable. What we mean by being *adaptable* is simply being able to make adjustments when the frustrations of parenting creep in. We've never said that raising kids was easy, but parents who are constantly on the lookout for better ways to do things tend to get more enjoyment out of life.

In our marriage, Chris is more of a routine person, and more of a morning person, too. He remembers waking up as a child to parents who enjoyed a couple hours of conversation before the day started. Early in our marriage, Chris tried to convert me (Wendy)—and I sincerely tried to oblige—to rise at the break of day and enjoy serene mornings together.

After a couple years of struggling to keep me awake with stronger coffee, Chris came up with a great idea: "How about you sleep in," he said, "and I'll get the household going in the morning." Nowadays, Chris enjoys his 5 a.m. mornings and makes the kids' breakfast about 7:00. Chris (or one of the kids) then brings me a cup of coffee in bed. After breakfast and devotions, I am out of bed and in the shower. Chris sends the kids to do their chores before leaving for the office. By the time I am out of the shower and dressed, the kids are well on with their chores and I am wide awake, ready to take on the day.

It took us a few years to settle on this routine, but it works very well now. We've seen families struggle to establish their own routine, but if a couple works together, they eventually do. Chris' parents have never deviated: they still wake up at 5 a.m. We know of another family that routinely stays up until 2 or 3 a.m. and starts home-schooling after lunchtime the next day.

Please don't make this more complicated than necessary. The concept is simple: Be creative enough and adaptable enough to discover the routine that best works for you. There is no *holy* schedule that every family should follow. We have heard arguments from well-intentioned people who claim that rising early is theologically more virtuous than sleeping in. They reference Proverbs 31:15, "She gets up while it is still dark…" and claim this means all mothers need to get up before the break of day. Curiously, these same people never seem to interpret the surrounding passages just as literally, or they would then proceed to feed their servants, select their wool and flax, plant a vineyard and make all their bed coverings and clothes from scratch. We won't tell you what time to wake up each morning, only that those mothers who adopt a routine that works for them are mothers whose children "arise and call her blessed" (Proverbs 31:28).

Still, there are times in life when we lose track of our routine and everything seems to fall apart. Those times are when it's more important than ever to remain adaptable. There are times Chris has an important project at work and needs to head to the office before the kids get up; sickness may take over the house and keep him up at night with a coughing child; other times Wendy will get up early and enjoy a conversation with her husband before the kids wake up; there are many occasions where Chris will stay up late and enjoy a conversation with his wife. Life is full of surprises, and remaining adaptable to those surprises is the logical thing to do.

Attitude Change #3: Blow off the trends, styles and cultural stereotypes.

As parents of 13 children, we have little patience for cultural taboos. Living up to societal expectations can be daunting, so do yourself a favor and don't bother trying. We're not saying to always "buck the system"; sometimes the system makes perfect sense. What we're saying is to trust in your ability to be creative in your home—creative with your schedule, your parenting, your everything—and don't let cultural attitudes thwart that creativity.

I (Chris) grew up with three sisters and no brothers, so I have no problem handling more "feminine" tasks that many men avoid. When shopping at Wal-Mart with the TLC crew trailing us, Wendy agreed to go through the checkout line with the first round of groceries while I took the kids to the clothing department to shop for party outfits. The male producer stopped me and asked, "Why are you choosing to shop for clothes—typically the woman's job—instead of heading through the register?" Without missing a beat, I said, "Because the kids need clothes," and I left it at that. Another day I was washing dishes when the producer asked why I was washing dishes instead of Wendy. "I am the father of 13 children," I said. "My masculinity is not threatened by doing a few dishes." We were disappointed that these lines were edited from the final program (all due to time constraints) because they illustrate how we've ignored cultural expectations in pursuit of God's plan for our family.

That trip to Wal-Mart was the only time during the year when we took the kids shopping for clothes. This was in preparation for our annual Jeub Birthday Bash (a tradition explained in the next chapter), for which we buy a new outfit for every child. Throughout the rest of the year, we are given hundreds of outfits to sort through. Our family has neither the time nor the desire (or the money) to keep pace with fashion trends. Yet we have many friends who do, and when their clothes become slightly out of style, they pass them onto us. We are grateful for these give-away items, and we don't pay attention to the cultural attitude that says this somehow makes us second-class. Even if our income was 10 times what it is now, we still would gladly accept someone else's spring-cleaning leftovers.[7]

Attitude is Everything

These three attitudes are essential for every parent: *God will provide, be adaptable,* and *throw off cultural expectations.* In the next chapter, we will explain how parenting is a daily exercise in creativity.

Chapter 4

Clutter, Shopping, Traveling and Birthdays

When a family applies the three attitude changes covered in the previous chapter—recognizing that God provides, remaining adaptable and disregarding cultural expectations—parents discover the freedom that allows for more children. Freedom is a valuable commodity, and we explore this further in our chapter on freedom. For now, let's look at some creative ideas that make life more enjoyable for families of all sizes.

Household Clutter

De-cluttering was a major accomplishment for me (Wendy) about four kids ago, when I discovered a most wonderful lady who goes by the name "FlyLady" (see www.flylady.com). Like a fairy godmother, FlyLady sends out regular emails reminding subscribers when to attack their clutter, when to dust, when to clean, and so on. Her articles and emails were a great encouragement for me and my clutter-prone personality.

We all know mothers for whom cleaning comes naturally. I am not one of them. Some of my dearest friends have immaculate homes, but I don't believe it is because they have fewer kids. The women I'm thinking of would have neat homes even with a dozen kids. They take great pleasure in grabbing a broom or a washcloth. I envy these friends!

FlyLady helped me structure my days. She answered questions I didn't even think to ask. When, for example, should I make the bed? Before taking a shower or after? When should Mom take a shower? (I used to shower around 3 in the afternoon, when I felt grimy and slimy and couldn't stand it any longer.) And when was a good time to clean the bathroom? (In theory, when it was messy. In reality, never.)

FlyLady presented a logical routine, with simple advice that makes an incredible amount of sense. When is the best time to make the bed? When I get out of it. The bathroom is cleaned when the shower is exited. And what about the dinner dishes? You guessed it: *after dinner*.

Following FlyLady's advice is like drinking deeply from a water jug of truth. Our laundry area is a small room in the basement. Chris built a laundry chute as a creative solution to the annoying hassle of overflowing laundry baskets all over the house. The resulting pile of dirty clothes is very intentional—one centralized mess as opposed to little messes all over the house. Lydia (our present laundry changer) sorts the laundry into baskets on a shelf until the pile is orderly. The clothes from the dryer are brought upstairs and folded. There's no organization involved in this, just the will to do it. We fold clothes, but not baby bibs or washcloths. If socks aren't already matched, we throw them in our "miss-made" basket (an entire hamper of socks) in the hope of matching them in the near future.

We've met people who had horrific notions of what the laundry must be like in our home. They find it hard to believe that handling the laundry takes only about 30 minutes at the start of each day. We remove the clothes from the dryer and pass them to a child to fold and put away. Because doing laundry is now a matter of routine, we're more aware of the laundry cycle and much more likely to return for another round later in the day. The creative routine keeps clothes clean, sorted and put away.

Shopping

We are often asked, "How much do you spend on groceries?" Most parents imagine a basic mathematical equation: Their Average Cost per Child x 13 Children = The Jeubs' Grocery Bill. Yet without fail, our grocery bill is usually half or less of what most parents spend on just one child! Specifically, we spend less than $600 per month on our groceries. How can this be?

This is where Attitude Change #3 comes into play: Disregard cultural expectations. Our family rarely buys brand names when a generic is available. When another family offers us charity—whether food, clothes, furniture, or any kind of help—we gratefully accept. We're certainly not scavengers (remember Attitude #1: God provides), but when someone offers help, we're open to receive. Fran Hanus, the mother of 14 first mentioned in Chapter 1, expressed the same philosophy when we visited her home a year ago. "When someone offers you their blessing," she told us, "refusing it is actually refusing God's gifts." Fran and Michael have always maintained a loose hold on their pocketbook, and though they've never been well off financially, they are richly blessed when it comes to what matters most: faith, family and friends.

It comes to some as a surprise that we have never in our married life been on food stamps.[8] Because of the number of children we have, we are technically in "poverty," as the government defines it. In fact, we are very close to the line defined as "extreme poverty." Yet, our needs are met in abundance! We believe the reasons are threefold: (1) God provides for our needs, (2) we accept generous offers from others, and (3) we deliberately look for good deals.

This third reason can become a book itself. Creative solutions are all around us and we're constantly on the lookout for them. We know all the best deals at Sam's Club and Wal-Mart, we shop at Safeway nearly every week for the blow-out items, and we get a Sunday paper simply to stay abreast to the deals. Why everyone doesn't do this, we can't say. We have in our married life together been much more impoverished than we are now, but we aren't any less investigative of neighborhood deals than we were then. Who knows, if we made six-figures we likely would be just as frugal!

There are many creative ways to save money. I (Wendy) have gathered several frugal tips over the years. Here are some that you could apply immediately to keep your budget down:

- Bring a calculator when you shop to pound out weight/cost conversions.
- If there is a generic substitute, get it. We rarely buy brand names.
- Buying bulk *usually* brings the price down, so do the math to make sure.
- Shop according to price per weight, not lowest overall price.
- Before buying a prepared meal ask, "Could this be cheaper if I make it myself?"
- Buy concentrated soaps and cleaning supplies, and make them stretch.
- Pour a couple more cups of water into your concentrated juice.
- Chill on the organic diet. Organics are expensive, so be choosy.
- Garden. Though it isn't feasible for us to garden where we now live due to high altitude and poor soil, we gardened and canned *a lot* when we lived in Minnesota.
- Search out the day-old food. Produce and bakery are typically marked down considerably when there is excess.

- Search out sales on meat. Buy large quantities and freeze for future use.
- When you shop, prepare a shopping list ahead of time — then stick to it.
- Don't go shopping *hungry.*
- Marry a guy who hunts.

I laugh at the last one, but it makes more sense than people realize. Chris isn't necessarily a fervent hunter, but he does go elk hunting once a year. He and his friends typically bring home elk and we together process the meat into steaks, roasts and burger. We mentioned earlier in the book that we rarely—if ever—buy steaks in the supermarket, but this doesn't mean we don't enjoy good steaks throughout the year. Most people wouldn't think twice paying over $10 a pound for some steaks, but we sure do. We eat like kings for a fraction of the cost.

There is no shortage of books on the subject of frugality. One of our friends, Ellie Kay, a mother of seven children, has honed her financial creativity as the wife of a military officer. Ellie's books include *A Mom's Guide to Family Finances* and *How to Save Money Every Day.* Her latest title, *Half-Price Living,* teaches readers how to adopt a lifestyle that allows for one parent to stay home with the kids. Her tips are invaluable for families who need to get by on a small budget.

Not surprisingly, Ellie has a special affinity for military families. Her book *Heroes at Home* describes how military families struggle financially and—by applying the methods in her book—civilian families can help. This is an important application of creative saving and spending: We need to have generous hearts—both within our families and with others. Remember that financial control offers freedom to own and freedom to give. We are cheerful givers, and we look at our thriftiness as a creative way to continue giving.

Traveling

When Wendy and I first got married, our family vehicle was a 1980 Chevette. It didn't take long to grow into a 4-door sedan, then a minivan, then a 9-seat Suburban, and finally a 15-passenger van. God has always enabled us to pay cash for each vehicle, and He has taught us to be creative when it comes to traveling. Because we consistently ignore cultural expectations—and because our 15-passenger van was busting at the seams—we did something that was incredibly—yet creatively—out of the norm: We bought a school bus.

This "crazy" idea of owning a bus came from a bigger family than ours. During the summer of 2003, we hosted a family with 16 children, the Heppners, for two weeks. The Heppners were one of the three families that appeared on "Kids by the Dozen", and were responsible for referring a number of other large families to TLC—including ours. "Kids by the Dozen" featured three families from different parts of the country, but never indicated that the families knew each other. The Heppners, however, are very good friends of ours.

DuWayne and Miriam Heppner brought 12 of their children with them to Colorado that summer (we had only 10 at the time). They traveled in a school bus, and DuWayne insisted that I (Chris) get behind the wheel. It was quite a trip we took to the local ice cream parlor—me in the front with 20-plus kids in the back! Needless to say, I was impressed by how easy the bus handled and how comfortable the kids were. After that first test drive, we began shopping for one to own. We were soon the proud owners of a 1984 GMC 65-passenger bus with only 40,000 miles on it. And we paid just $1,200. With the typical RV priced at well over $50,000, cost was a very compelling reason to go the bus route!

While price definitely played a role, there were many other reasons for buying a bus. First was flexibility. Our website includes the story of how we converted the Jeub Family Bus (www.jeubfamily.com/bus). The bus conversion community is an incredible group of creative people who transform gutted-out school buses into the mobile homes of their dreams. We have met missionary families who treated their bus conversion as a means for transporting Christian resources to Mexico and Central America. We've met other families who travel the country in their converted bus operating a business. Still others are families like ours that are simply looking for a recreational vehicle to haul around a bunch of kids. When you purchase a school bus—raw and ready to convert—you have all the flexibility in the world to create the vehicle you want.

The second creative reason for purchasing our "schoolie" was simply to have *fun.* Owning and converting our bus has been an incredible adventure. The kids helped out during every step of the process, from cleaning to modeling to painting. A trip to the mountains has never been more enjoyable than with our bus. The kids play games at the dinettes while Wendy and I take turns caring for the little ones on the couch. We have driven to Minnesota for a family reunion and to Missouri for a wedding, and we always make time for tourist stops along the way. Every so often we take the bus to church, making all our kids' friends wish their families owned a bus, too!

Our decision to purchase a bus also made practical sense. Any serious traveling in a 15-passenger van is incredibly confining with a family our size. Most RVs are designed for families of 2-4 kids, not 13. When you think about it, owning a bus isn't that silly at all. As one dad shared with us: "I am a truck driver for a living. I see families like yours driving down the highway and I usually think, 'They're crazy!' But now that I have actually met one, I think to myself, 'Who are the crazy ones here?' I strap my kids in the minivan, cram it full of luggage, and we drive each other crazy on long trips. If anything is crazy, that is!"

We laughed at his humor, but his logic rang true. Our bus has taken our family on many adventures these last three years, so many that we can't imagine traveling long distances without it. Sure, we get strange looks sometimes, but we are convinced that God has used our bus to give us adventures we wouldn't have discovered otherwise.

Birthdays

When parents embrace creative solutions to their frustrations, family life becomes a lot more enjoyable. One "point of pain" that grew as our family expanded was how to handle birthday parties. Relatives couldn't make it to town for every child's birthday, and we weren't crazy about the idea of planning a dozen parties every year. The expectation for most parents is to host a celebration—or some formal recognition—of each child's birthday. We like this tradition, but as our family grew, our enthusiasm faded.

In 1998 we thought of a solution, and the more we pondered it, the more we liked it. The idea was born out of economic necessity: If we spent, say, $75 per child for each birthday, we would end up spending over $400 every year. Instead, what if we had just one big birthday party per year? The idea was appealing, but we still had our doubts.

Would we be cheating our kids out of their special day? All the parents we know have some sort of party for each of their kids. Individual birthday parties are a cultural expectation in our church and community. Needless to say, our kids weren't that crazy about the idea, either. Children naturally want to enjoy a birthday celebration of their own. That's why, though we may have reduced the number of parties, we still recognize each child's special day. The birthday boy or girl still gets breakfast in bed (the rest of the family cooks and prepares) and individual gifts from siblings and parents. They also get their choice of meal, followed by a simple birthday cake and ice cream. No big party, no big expense. We save that for our big once-a-year bash!

The kids eventually caught the vision for this single birthday party, and we dubbed it the annual *Jeub Birthday Bash*. Our first Bash was a raving success: About 50 friends and relatives turned out for a day of food, games, presents and fellowship. A friend brought his horses for the kids to ride and we shared marshmallows around a campfire in the backyard. The party was a great amount of fun, and the kids were sold on the idea.

Today, our kids look forward to the Jeub Birthday Bash like they anticipate Christmas or Easter. The event has since grown to include face painting, a piñata, homemade root beer, a treasure hunt and games galore. And there's always someone willing to help with the horseback rides. Feeding our ever-expanding guest list isn't easy, but every year we make it work.

The 2006 Bash was the central event in our "Kids by the Dozen" episode. Lots of planning and preparation goes into a successful Jeub Birthday Bash. Shopping, cooking and cleaning are already major tasks for a family of our size, but we were shopping, cooking and cleaning for an expected 150 people—with a camera crew in tow. In the end, nearly 190 people (kids and adults) attended the day-long celebration. Not only do our kids look forward to the Birthday Bash, evidently their friends do, too. (As do ours!)

The Jeub Birthday Bash is just one example of using our God-given creativity to benefit our family. These days, our kids can't imagine life without the Bash. We have to explain to the younger ones who don't remember life without it that other children don't have a Birthday Bash. We can't imagine trying to "keep up" with the cultural expectation of throwing a birthday party for every child. Our kids, too, are glad to give up downsized individual parties in exchange for our huge Bash. The party has become a group effort that brings our entire family closer together.

Complicated schedules, tight budgets, individual preferences, community expectations, and common annoyances affect families of all sizes. Allowing these factors to control our life is much more exhausting than tapping into our creative juices and coming up with solutions to these frustrations. In this chapter we shared four common frustrations—managing stuff, shopping, traveling and birthdays—that, over time, took creativity to make them the enjoyable things they should be. We believe every family has the ability to come up with creative solutions to any problem that comes their way. In fact, we have found that these solutions—especially true with the examples of our bus and the Jeub Birthday Bash—have themselves brought much joy into our family life.

Chapter 5

Choosing to Be Free

God has created us to enjoy a life of freedom within His will, but many people choose to live in what we refer to as "bondage." Those who consider children a strain on their freedom don't really understand how having children can lead to incredible freedom. We are convinced that children are a blessing from God and, if parents embrace the right perspective, can be a liberating antidote to many cultural misconceptions.

Although we have lived it for many years, we fully grasped this concept only recently. When the TLC crew stayed at our home, the producer caught us off guard simply by quoting our own words. "You keep describing yourself as *free*," he said. "Why do you keep saying that?"

We struggled at first to find the right words for the cameras. (Much of what we said ended up on the editing floor, so we're not totally sure what exactly came out.) We spoke of being financially free because we strive to stay out of debt. Chris spoke of how self-employment brings freedom, and Wendy spoke of being free to love our children. It was a strange feeling: We often referred to "freedom" when describing our way of life, yet when given the chance to nail down the definition, our tongues were tied.

Freedom is, essentially, the concept that Jesus Christ explicitly tried to impart to his followers: “It is for freedom that Christ has set us free. Stand firm, then, and do not let yourselves be burdened again by a yoke of slavery.”[9] Our message to young couples who are struggling with the decision to have children is one of freedom. While so many cultural messages attempt to persuade couples that children are a form of bondage, our life is evidence that we are free, blessed with opportunity and quite happy with 13 children. (And we would welcome even more!)

There exists an irritated opposition to our views on freedom, especially the freedom of bearing children. Some couples claim to find freedom in *not* being parents. They travel, they dive into their careers, they appear perfectly fulfilled with their single lives. Some are quite rude about our choices. These couples join “childless by choice” clubs that boast of the wonderful freedoms they enjoy when they don’t have kids to weigh them down. They build websites devoted to “the childfree life,” posting quotes, articles and interesting facts of how the world has been “blessed” by the absence of more children. They clearly view children as a form of bondage.

It is this last point that we *must* challenge. Be assured that it isn’t *not* bearing children that leads to bondage; the deeper issue is fleeing from God in rebellion. Ignoring God’s plan for your life—whether that plan is celibacy without children or marriage with many—will lead only to disappointment and frustration. You will not experience freedom; you will experience misery.

The freedom we speak of is a freedom that allows God to bless us with what He chooses. Rather than seeking to do our own thing, impelled by society's misguided notions of fulfillment, we are *free* to seek *His* will and *resting* in it. We don't wrestle with the issue of reproduction each time we have a child, as most of society and many Christians do. We are quite content with God blessing us as He sees fit, and we have seen time and time again God providing for our needs when He gives us another child. After 13 validations of God's wonderful blessings, why would we think we live a life of bondage?

It is quite a modern phenomenon that views children as a form of bondage. The Childless by Choice crowd looks at materialism as the ultimate blessing. Wealth and travel, social status and fame—these are the virtues of the child-free modernists. And children are nothing but a nuisance.

Compare this perspective with the heart of Abram, the patriarch of the Jewish faith, who, after 70 years of faithfully serving God, was disappointed with the results. What were those results? On a materialistic level, they were quite impressive:

Wealth and travel: "Lift up your eyes from where you are and look north and south, east and west. All the land that you see I will give to you and your offspring forever." (Genesis 13:15)

Social status and fame: "I will make you into a great nation and I will bless you; I will make your name great and you will be a blessing." (Genesis 12:2)

Abram was indeed blessed. He had hundreds of servants, was highly respected among the people, and enjoyed complete financial independence. Abram seemingly had nothing to complain about. He was a *GQ* kind of guy; the total package.

Yet Abram did have *one* problem: *He had no children...*

> Abram said, "O Sovereign Lord, what can you give me since I remain childless and the one who will inherit my estate is Eliezer of Damascus?" And Abram said, "You have given me no children; so a servant in my household will be my heir." (Genesis 15:2-3)

Abram recognized back then what so many fail to see today. A modernist sees a child as a curse; a righteous man (Abram was accredited as "righteous") sees a child as a blessing. A modernist sees little value in passing on a heritage to his offspring; a righteous man sees great value in building up a heritage to pass on. A modernist sees life with children as inconvenient; a righteous man sees great value in life with children. The contrast is revealing.

God desires every person to seek His will. Our heart's desire is that every person (child-full or child-free) develops a passion for seeking God's will. "Conviction" is a beautiful term when it is fully understood. God's gentle prods are "convictions." They are not condemning judgments. When you get to know God through Jesus Christ, you open yourself to God's wonderful convictions. We don't pretend to know everyone's personal convictions, so we aren't about to say that *everyone* should have as many children as possible. We will never challenge anyone who feels a conviction from God to refrain from having children, if that is what they truly believe. However, we will challenge anyone who puts personal ambitions ahead of God's plan in their life.

We have plenty of experience when it comes to God's conviction. It comes as a surprise to many people that when we were still relatively young in our marriage, we became adamant about *not* having any more children. I (Chris) was a teacher, and we already had more children—four—than any other family in our entire school district. That's when Wendy gave birth to our first boy, Isaiah, and modern wisdom told us we were finished. After four girls, we finally had our son. Why burden ourselves with more children?

Thus began the most trying time of our reproductive lives. All worldly reason—from both Christian and non-Christian circles—told us to start using birth control, but God was relentless in convicting us to have more children. We heard all the arguments against more kids: Chris wouldn't have enough time for his students. Wendy wouldn't have time to do anything around the house. The older kids wouldn't be able to enjoy their adolescence, and the younger kids would naturally be ignored.

Do you see how "logical" it all sounds? How it makes perfect sense that increasing the number of people in a household would only increase the responsibilities, the duties, the grocery bill, the need for work, the insurance, etc., etc.?

The most challenging arguments came from Christian friends who, some subtle and some not, said we were irresponsible for having so many children. Yet this was in direct contradiction to what we felt God was laying on our hearts. Through it all, our sense of conviction never changed: *Keep having children.* We can't explain it more clearly than that. Whenever we prayed for another answer, God patiently convinced us that we weren't done yet.

How Parenting Brings Freedom

The frustrating reality is that couples today simply cannot fathom a life with children as *free.* So let's examine some misconceptions people often have about family life, misconceptions especially true to large families like ours. You will see that most of these misconceptions have to do with one's perception of freedom. The blessing of children is exactly that—a *blessing*. And blessings don't lead to bondage.

Parenting limits my ability to travel

Sure, we sometimes wonder what it would be like to take a luxurious trip to a foreign country, but our attitude is that our day will come. That's not to say that we don't travel, but our trips are usually centered on family events like reunions and weddings. That's okay with us, because we are enjoying the child-producing years right now and we know that they won't last forever.

Whenever Wendy and I notice an older couple out enjoying a motorcycle ride, we grin and say, "That's you and me someday!" You see, I (Chris) have always wanted a motorcycle. A few years ago I had an opportunity to buy one, and Wendy actually agreed to the idea! However, our house was full of little kids, not young adults who could actually enjoy the motorcycle with me. So we decided to postpone the idea of owning a motorcycle until a day when we can include the entire family in the fun.

Does parenting limit your ability to travel? If traveling means the flexibility to fly off to remote parts of the world in a snap, then we would have to agree that yes, parenting does limit things. But we see traveling as a wonderful opportunity to experience other places *with* our children. Our view of traveling is enjoyable *as a family*.

All my money will go into my children

We've all heard the dire predictions from sociologists or demographers: "A child born today will cost his or her parents $632,000 by the time they graduate from high school." Faced with such daunting numbers, it's easy to understand why a young couple would rather save all that money and travel around the world. New parents are especially vulnerable to this logic as they see how much of their income goes toward disposable products like baby clothes, food and diapers.

We suppose we are still in those heavy-spending years, but there will come a day when our children will be productive adults. They will give back to our family and to society. We're not saying they will literally pay back their parents monetarily, but they will give back in other ways. We know this to be true because we've seen this principle in action. The other two families featured on TLC's "Kids by the Dozen" both benefit greatly from the contributions of their grown children. DuWayne Heppner, a father of 16, today enjoys the equivalent of a small construction crew. Rick Arndt, too, has all 14 children still at home to help with the family businesses and work on their homestead. The Arndts and the Heppners are about a decade ahead of us. We currently have 11 kids 14 and under—hardly a productive crew. However, the day will come when we will have 11 kids ages 16-30. Now those will be productive years!

I will not be able to put time into my other children if I have too many

There is some truth to this. We are not able to give each child a lot of individual attention. We certainly try to maximize the time we spend with our kids, but the reality is that *quantity* time is definitely limited the more children we have.

We'd like to challenge two ideas. First has to do with the idea that the amount of time parents spend with each child is fundamentally important. There is an added component with large families that small families can never replicate: a robust population of *siblings*. We will talk more about this later in the book, but for now it is worth noting that children in large families develop a powerful and long-lasting social bond with each other. Yet many parents continue to think of themselves as the only determining need in their children's lives.

Please don't misunderstand us: We are not suggesting that parents neglect their children, or that kids don't benefit from a parent's time and attention. What we are saying is that limiting your family's size is not necessarily the best thing for the children you already have. And cutting short your reproductive years shouldn't be interpreted as a blessing to your other kids.

Our second challenge is this: you can always think of creative ways to spend time with each child, even in a household of a dozen. This freedom is embedded in the busiest schedules. I (Wendy) appoint a "special helper" every week for cooking dinner. I take this time to teach the ins and outs of cooking as well as laugh and enjoy one another's company. When I (Chris) run errands during the week, I will often take a child with me to spend the time together, one-on-one. There may be limited minutes in a day, but there is not a limit to creative solutions that will, indeed, make time for individual children.

I will not have time for personal growth

Of all the arguments against large families, this one is the easiest to refute. There is nothing that will foster more personal growth than the raising of a child. You hear them say "dada" or "mama" for the first time. You help them to walk, then talk, then run. You're there when they start school, when they fight, when they cry, when they laugh and when they want to cuddle. You help them through their formative teenage years and on to adulthood. We can hardly imagine life without the challenging and highly dynamic presence of all our children.

Choosing God's Plan

Here is a simple exercise: The next time you are questioning how many children you should have, try replacing the word "children" with "God's blessings." Would you agree to any of the following statements?

- God's blessings will keep us from traveling as much as we want.
- God's blessings will cost us a lot of money.
- We will not be able to give our full attention to God's blessings.
- God's blessings will hinder our personal growth.

Do you feel the conviction, as we have, to have more children? If you do, resisting that conviction is essentially agreeing to the statements above. Worse yet, imagine saying these statements to God in prayer. "God, your blessings will hinder our personal growth."

We know our message isn't an easy one for many couples. We certainly don't want to assume anyone's convictions and we don't want to assume God's will, but we must challenge the *intentional avoidance* of a heartfelt conviction to have more children. Based on feedback we've received over the years as we have shared our own story, the intentional avoidance of having children is a common regret in Christian families. Granted, we have been told by some couples that they do not share in the same conviction to have more children. That's fine. However, many couples have admitted to us of limiting their family size and later regretting their choice.

We believe God wants couples to enjoy the freedoms of family life. Procreation is one of many areas about which God has a lot to say—if a couple is willing to listen. Opening your heart to God's plans—including His plan for the number of children you have—is a liberating choice that leads to a fruitful and enjoyable life. If you and your spouse sense that conviction, we encourage you to find confidence in having another child.

Chapter 6

When Parenting Becomes Bondage

It's no secret that we are advocates for having children, but it's also true that we have met some miserable parents. There are those who insist on downplaying the joys of parenting. For example, I (Chris) recall sitting with three of our kids on a shuttle bus at a ski resort in Colorado when a mother sitting with two children struck up a conversation with a couple of college-aged men. This mother (within earshot of her kids) proclaimed: "Enjoy your life while you can! Once you have children, everything gets so difficult. What I would give to be young again!"

I remember this so well because the two students—whom you might expect to chime right in and complain about children—brushed off this mother's advice. One long-haired snowboarder said, "I believe children are a blessing." His friend agreed, "Yeah, I look forward to having a family." So much for stereotypes.

Encounters like this give us hope for our culture. These snowboarders, young and seemingly carefree, nonetheless recognized the undeniable value of family and children. Indeed, we know several women who grew up with extreme feminist goals only to undergo a 180-degree shift after having their first child. And rare is the man so filled with testosterone that he won't cuddle with his newborn daughter. All the crafty rhetoric in the world will not bring down the eternal truth of love, family and procreation.

Nevertheless, we often observe parents who've turned raising children into a chore, making everyone miserable in the process. We invited some new friends over for the first time, and as is our custom, I (Chris) gave them a tour of our six-acre property. It was a gorgeous day, and while the Mrs. stayed inside with Wendy, the Mr. and his daughter joined me outside (along with half of my kids). Our friend's daughter asked politely for permission every time my kids started a new activity.

"Can I jump on the trampoline?" she asked.

"No, maybe later," her dad replied.

"May I take my shoes off and walk in the creek?"

"Absolutely not, honey."

"Can I run through the trails with Mr. Jeub's kids?"

"No, stay by me."

We've all heard the saying, "Better to ask for forgiveness than permission," right? Before long, our friend's daughter began sneaking away from her father, doing things she knew her father would not approve. She stopped asking for permission. When parents do not clearly define boundaries for their children, frustration soon follows. Our friend began telling his daughter not to do things that she already started. "Don't pet the chickens … Don't let the dog lick your face … Don't jump too high on the trampoline … Stay close to me … Don't go too far …"

This was almost comical, because in the meantime our children were carrying the chickens, wrestling with the dog, having a heyday on the trampoline and running free with a joy to which we have grown accustomed. It soon became apparent that our friend was growing as frustrated as his daughter. "Honey, I told you to stay close … You're going to hurt yourself … Don't you see how dangerous this is? … We talked about this already, didn't we? … If you keep arguing with me, you're going to get in trouble!"

We hope you see the digression here. It is a downward spiral that happens so easily in parenting:

1. Child asks; parent says no.
2. Child stops asking; parent belatedly defines what is not allowed.
3. Child disobeys; parent disciplines.

Of these three, one is unavoidable: number three. When a child disobeys, we must address it—no doubt about that. However, numbers one and two could have easily been avoided. Our friend had gotten into the habit of denying his daughter's requests, to which he consistently responded by saying no. When his daughter, old enough to conclude there was no harm in what she was asking, started to do what she knew her father would not allow, the issue became one of obedience, not freedom. Our friend was compelled to confront issues of the heart—disobedience and disrespect. Too bad he couldn't reserve such a confrontation for much more worthy situations.

Really, do you want your children to always stay close to you, asking permission to do even the littlest thing, always afraid to try something new? No, you don't. Neither did our friend wish the same for his daughter, but that's where he and so many other parents end up.

We were in much the same situation early on in our parenting, but today we catch ourselves more often than not. We no longer fall into saying *no* as a knee-jerk response. We've learned to make freedom a joy in our household, and we urge you to do the same. We think you will find that when your children exercise freedom like they should—responsibly and respectfully—they will develop an independence that will make you proud.

However, we need to ask ourselves the same questions every parent should ask before saying no. These questions follow the three stated earlier:

1. The child asks. Instead of automatically saying *no*, we ask ourselves, "Is there a good reason to say *no*? What harm would come in my child doing what he is asking? Is there an alternative that would fulfill his request?"
2. The child doesn't ask. We ask ourselves, "Did I lay out reasonable boundaries for my child? Did I give my child permission to do anything in the first place?

Is she truly 'sneaking,' or just enjoying her freedom?"

3. The child disobeys. We address the disobedience with loving correction.

Children who are given appropriate freedom from a parent in steps one and two rarely make it to step three. Sure, sometimes they do, and our chapter on bringing order to chaos addresses when discipline is needed in child rearing. But being able to properly grant freedoms to your children will keep discipline from becoming the routine consequence of enjoyment.

How could our friend have done a better job? "Pet the chickens, but don't pick them up," he could have said. "Yes, you may walk in the creek, but don't splash." "Jump on the trampoline, but don't push the others around." Allowing his daughter a bit more freedom would have resulted in a lot of fun—good, safe fun—rather than a frustrated little girl who started to rebel because her father always said no.

Freedom. Value it greatly and teach it to your children.

Practical Applications: Being Free

The fact that having children is liberating—rather than enslaving—is a difficult concept to grasp. Truthfully, it took us several years to release ourselves from such subtle persuasions. When addressing people who are convinced that children are a form of bondage, we explain that bondage comes in many different forms, but children aren't one of them. It's taken us years to work through the following issues, but we've managed to confound the skeptics who are convinced that our family life must be characterized by chaos and exhaustion.

Economic Freedom

Money is a huge issue especially for young families. God knows that. While couples insist on restricting their family size because of economic fears, we see economics as one of the easiest obstacles to conquer. Economics is a bigger topic than this chapter can ever begin to cover, but we can't emphasize enough how important it is for a young couple to understand true economic freedom in their marriage, their job and their lifestyle..

First, parents can free themselves from the idea that there is a certain wage that the family needs to earn in order to "get by." We know of large families who earn half our salary and we know of large families who make 10 times what we do. We don't make *wealth* a criterion for having children. Even though children are born into richness and poverty alike, they are always blessings to those around them, especially their parents.

In fact, *money matters little.* This is a radical perspective, yet extremely liberating. When we pray, "Give us this day our daily bread," we seriously believe that God will provide for our daily needs. We are far from financially secure, but our security is not dependent on our finances. Our family history is replete with one story after another of how God has always provided for our needs, even during the tightest of times.

We are saddened when we hear of couples who choose to limit their family size just so they can build a bigger home (or second home), enjoy exotic vacations, or pay for gathering bills. Don't misread what we are saying—financial stewardship is definitely important—but stewardship certainly shouldn't limit the size of your family. If debt is an issue, learn to spend less. If materialism is an issue, sell your boat. If you can't balance your checkbook, see a financial counselor. There is no good reason to make finances a priority over family.

Second, most parents (especially fathers) feel the need to work outside the home to provide for their family. This is often due to a perceived standard of living these parents insist on achieving, but sometimes it is simply because they have not considered the alternatives. For example, when you own your own business, you are your own boss and your own provider. We made the scary move into self-employment three years ago, and everyday we see the blessing in the freedoms we now enjoy (including the freedom to write this book!).

Societal Freedom

Society imposes a host of expectations on young couples that, we believe, should be questioned. Indeed, we have rubbed some people the wrong way simply because we questioned a popular or "traditional" approach to parenting. We don't accept the idea that there is a purist or fundamentally superior way to raise children. Parents are free to reasonably choose what is best for their family.

We don't want to come across as nonconforming revolutionaries, but our life story is riddled with examples of bucking the system. We started home schooling our kids back when Chris was a public school teacher. We had one fellow teacher label us as religious fanatics, but we were convinced that home schooling was the best choice for our children. We have very healthy kids largely because Wendy refuses to shove antibiotics down their throats at every sign of a sniffle or sneeze. Several years ago we decided not to send our kids to Sunday school during the worship service (we felt God calling us to sit together as a family), and the church leadership kept our membership on hold because we apparently thought there was something wrong with *their* children.

Societal expectations can seriously hinder your ability as parents. We home school not because we're nonconformists, but because we believe it is a wonderful way to educate our children. We resist antibiotics because we know they can reduce a child's immune system (and many medical professionals agree). We keep our kids with us in church because we value worshiping together as a family.

Heaven forbid if we (or this book) suggest that there is a secret formula for parenting. We've simply resisted the societal persuasions to conform and made the best decisions we could at the time. It's not a secret formula, but it's worked out well for us.

Eternal Freedom

Of all we've learned in raising 13 kids, we need to make one thing perfectly clear: *Our parenting techniques amount to nothing without God as our leader and our Lord.* The Jeub family loves the Lord and the relationship we have with God through Christ, and we are compelled to display this love in front of the TLC cameras, on our Web site, and through the ink on this page.

Some people reading this book may think that faith in God is a trivial matter. But faith cannot be so easily brushed aside. We often wonder how folks who do not have a relationship with God can manage at all. When you trust in God and seek his direction, you discover that He is willing and eager to guide you. We didn't choose a life of 13 children on a mere whim. No, we are acting in obedience to God and the calling he has placed in our hearts. If we had never surrendered our desires to the Lord years ago, we would likely be running after worldly pleasures—as empty as those pleasures are.

Eternal freedom is the gift God offers to everyone. This means accepting Christ, allowing God to teach you His will for your life, and enjoying the ride. This ultimate freedom gives purpose to every so-called "choice" we make in life. Over the years, we have witnessed many parents surrender their reproductive lives to the will of God. Some are more gung-ho than others, some wanting a family as large as ours and some shaking with fear over the possibility. But *never* have we seen these same parents regret the blessings that follow that surrender. Children follow—and growth, love and freedom along with them.

Chapter 7

Bringing Order to the Chaos

A decade ago when most of our children were young, suppertime was as tremulous as a tornado. Cynthia, 5, would constantly get up from the table for a variety of reasons—going to the bathroom, getting a drink, dropping her silverware, *whatever*. Lydia, two years younger, would follow each time. Isaiah, 1, would shout from his highchair for anything on the table that was not already on his tray. We would try desperately to find the items he pointed at. The frustrated older children would be told what to do from equally frustrated parents: "Get a towel, give him some ketchup, sit down!"

Been there? The evening dinner ends with temper tantrums and high anxiety, a laundry basket full of wet towels from spilled drinks, and crying screams from both spanked children and frustrated older children. Hardly a pleasant meal with the kids!

It has been said that the strongest argument for birth control is children. Though children *should* be the joys of their parents, the truth is that children are often little devils that tear the house apart. All parents can find comfort that God will provide ways to help raise children. Back in the chaotic-dinnertime days, we were struggling to see how God could provide solutions to such a mess. Our conviction begged the question: How could we bring more children into the world when we couldn't even sit down to a meal together?

Today our dinnertime is a joy. We have many more than five kids. Chris makes the habit of spending at least one meal a day at home. Wendy sits on one side of the table with the twins in their highchairs. Chris sits on the other side with the main dishes within arm's reach to scoop up the food onto passing plates. Between us are nine other children sitting on two benches on each side of the table. This table is ten years old (we need to upgrade to a larger table soon), but it still surprises us how many kids we can fit with benches instead of chairs.

Everyone shares in conversation while we eat. Even our two-year-old sits on the bench without getting up and running around. When we take a baby out of a highchair to sit in our lap, the baby doesn't grab for our food and force us to clear a barren spot from his reach; the baby contently eats what we put in front of him. Our kids aren't jumping up from the table for anything other than forgotten items like an extra fork or salad dressing. Children who finish early sit patiently until everyone is finished eating. "May I be excused, Mommy?" is asked. This is often followed with eight other requests. The children take their plates, scrape them into the garbage, and proceed to their after-dinner chores.

Sound like a dream? You may be thinking that we're making this up, but we're not. We *love* to have meals together. It is one of the most enjoyable moments of our day. A meal ought to be an honoring time of the day for a mother and father. Why has it become a dreaded time for parents?

We believe such chaos is a result of parents failing to properly teach their children good behavior. Though it is common to brush it aside, parents must take the time to teach their children proper behavior. If your dinnertimes resemble what it was like for us a decade ago, this is perhaps the most practical and liberating chapter in this book.

Making Obedience a Game to Win

Dinnertime is only one example. Children should be able to sit through an hour long church service, should be able to accept "no" for their request for candy in a supermarket, and should be able to put away their toys when they are told. We were recently told of parents who would forcibly wrench their daughter into a car seat, and their daughter would proceed to scream at the top of her lungs *for the entire car trip*. Their answer, sadly, was to trade their minivan for a small RV to avoid having to strap their daughter in. These parents (who are much, much more intelligent than their 3-year-old) had given into their daughter's will. No doubt these young parents will likely think twice before having more children.

There are a number of solutions out there that could be had, but not every one would work. "That child needs a good spanking!" is certainly understandable, but it is very difficult to beat a child into sitting in a car seat. Besides, we have found that spanking a child for anything other than pure defiance to be largely unproductive. An anti-spanking advocate may argue, "You must reason with the child and discuss the benefits of sitting in a car seat." This 3-year-old is hardly able to reason, so I see this solution as even more ridiculous than the first.[10]

We have found the method of *practicing* proper behavior to be the best way to teach a child how to behave in critical situations. If, say, this 3-year-old was our daughter, we would set up a practice scenario for our 3-year-old to play in. We would take the car seat into the playroom. "We are going to practice going to the store!" we would say in a playful tone. The 3-year-old would get into her car seat as if it were a game, and we would drive with big happy faces to the store. Only a minute of driving is needed in a playful situation. We then would proceed to unbuckle our daughter and walk out of the playroom and into the pretend store. We may make-believe buying her a piece of candy for being so well behaved.

If this sounds silly, remember how ridiculous it is for two grown adults bending their daughter in half to buckle her up and tolerating blood-curdling screams all the way home. If there is anything a child understands more than getting what she wants, it is *play*, and playtime is a perfect solution to teaching a child proper behavior. Whenever we are met with an unpleasant situation in our household, we ask ourselves, "How can we practice the proper way to do this?"

We commonly run into an issue where the kids would be called from a distance, but they would choose to wait for a second or third call before responding. Virtually every parent in the world experiences at some point this "selective listening" from their children. Can you imagine tolerating this with a dozen children? Rather than reverting to yelling or punishments, we take some time to play a simple game. We sit the children on the couch and play "Yes Sir!" or "Yes Ma'am!" Call out the name of the child and let the child respond as quickly as possible. A big smile and hug from dad or mom is a great reward for being so responsive. Another game has been a cleanup game where our children will be at our side ready to pick up whatever we tell them. "Cynthia, put that basket in the boys' room; Tabitha, bring those socks to the laundry shoot; Isaiah, dump that garbage out…" and so on. With a dozen kids waiting for their next command, we can teach obedience while cleaning the house in no time flat!

Practicing Works Best

Practicing good behavior is much more effective than *punishing* a child into good behavior. In fact, we would argue that negative reinforcement alone is a poor teacher. We have witnessed homes where the parents are constantly spanking the children or (for any anti-spanking folks that may be reading this book) constantly placing their little devils in the corner for hours on end. When the child throws a fit—*wham!*—comes the rod. If the child doesn't respond the first three times they are called—*swish!*—off to the dreaded corner they go. These children are usually angry and frustrated if not timid and afraid, and the parents are typically a knotted up mess.

Such situations breed abuse. Whether it results in redder-than-needed bottoms or a child pounding his head into the corner of a wall, the abusive result is a frustrated child. Fathers are told explicitly in Ephesians chapter 6 to not "exasperate" their children. Constantly disciplining and punishing children creates more exasperation in a family, not less. In fact, fathers and mothers end up just as exasperated as their children! Ephesians 6:4 is a beautiful verse because it provides the solution as well as the admonition for parents to follow:

> Fathers, do not exasperate your children; instead, bring them up in the training and instruction of the Lord.

Notice the solutions: *training and instruction.* The solution for an exasperated child is not more spankings or punishments. When we find ourselves frustrated because we're exasperating our children, we take a breather and ask ourselves, "Have we been instructing our children on how to behave properly?" We then proceed to create practicing situations where the kids learn proper behavior. The exasperation and frustration disappears and the household returns to order.

The concept of practicing proper behavior works! Parents who take the time to practice proper behavior are parents who find their children to be the joys of their lives. Parents who do not take this time and result to parenting "from the hip" very typically lead frustrating, exhausting families.

One of the most popular verses in the bible used for parenting is most commonly misused: "Train up a child in the way he should go" (Proverbs 22:6). This is misused in two extremes. First, "train" is equated with "beat," and this verse is held up with equal weight as Proverbs 23:14, "Punish him with a rod and save his soul from death." Second, "train" is used as a substitute for corporal punishment, and the "rod" is loosely defined as some sort of administrative tool rather than clear corrective discipline. We've entertained both extremes, and in our years of parenting we have come to see that the best results come with a more functional approach to child rearing.

See, there is a role for discipline, but there is a bigger role for instruction. Too often parents will substitute their instruction with discipline, expecting children to respond properly like a horse responds to a whip. Teaching proper behavior ought to be at the forefront of parenting. If parents want to have households of happy kids, fewer spankings, enriched conversations and peaceful dinnertimes and evenings, practicing with the kids will be done often.

The next chapter will give practical ideas for *training and instructing*. Some have snickered at the idea of "training" children, as if we advocate treating children no smarter than pets. We don't think of our children as pets at all. Quite the contrary, we see our children as much more intelligent than our pets, and this actually *builds the case* to expect proper behavior from children. We see "training" in an educational sense, like children preparing for classroom behavior. There are certain things children—everyone, for that matter—need to adapt to and social expectations to follow. Our practices—as you will see in the next chapter—do not devalue or disrespect childhood. Our children are joyful, well socialized children, largely due to the practices we apply.

Chapter 8

Peaceful Church, Shopping and Bedtime

When a child misbehaves, the most common reaction from parents is discipline or punishment. We challenge parents to change that initial reaction. When our children misbehave—especially in public—our first reaction is to question whether we spent enough time teaching or practicing. This chapter lists three common situations with which most parents struggle and then gives solutions to bring peace to the family.

Church

Nowhere do we get more comments on how well behaved our children are than in church. Most parents have attempted to sit with their toddler or young child during an adult sermon only to end up in back sitting with (or on) their disruptive child. The scenario is common. Mom starts with her child sitting next to her. As the service begins, the child asks to sit on Mom's lap. Innocent enough, Mom complies, to which the child slouches and starts to kick the back of the pew with her noisy dress shoes. The child resists Mommy's correction and lets out unpleasant whines. The child proceeds to ask Mommy several questions—all of which have no other intention but to break the boredom of the church service: *can I get down, can I have a drink, I'm hungry, I need to go to the bathroom, etc.* Mommy probably took a couple of trips to the back before finally "having enough" (a relative breaking point all parents have). The child returns to Mommy's lap kicking the back of the pew. Mommy holds the child's leg down. The child attempts to kick beyond her mommy's strength. The child lets out a frustrated, crabby cry. Now the entire church has their attention on the mommy and her daughter, not the service. Instead of listening to the teaching from the Word of God, people are hoping for a shortened sermon. The frustrated Mommy slaps the child softly (yet with an audible *snap*) on her daughter's thigh. Half the congregation is appalled at the spanking, the other half is thinking, "It's about time." Mom picks up the child—by now screaming and wailing—and either throws her to Daddy (to start the process all over again) or stomps out the back of the church.

As a response to disruptive children, some churches simply do not allow families to sit together. We've been stopped at the door by the good intentions of ushers: "Excuse me, but the children must go down the hall to Children's Church." As already mentioned, we find great value in worshiping as a family, but we have often felt pressured to break the family up into age-appropriate pieces. Frankly, we can't blame churches for not allowing children in the sanctuary. Who wants to put up with a church full of situations like the one above?

When families *practice* church at home before attending church together, they find that sitting quietly in a church service can be a very enjoyable experience. Practically speaking, how do we practice church? In the hustle and bustle of Sunday morning, a dozen kids eating, bathing, dressing, and getting out to the van requires our full attention. Just as important as finding matching socks is taking the time to practice church. When a child is finished getting ready for church, we tell that child to go sit quietly on the sofa. When we first started this routine, Mom or Dad had to sit with the child to properly show him how to sit still and quiet. Today, the children have grown accustomed to the routine. Within about 15 minutes, we will have all our children lined up on our sofas. We reinforce verbally that "this is how we behave in church." We simply sit quietly together; the practice is not more complex than this. The littler kids may take some correction, but they adapt remarkably well to what their older siblings do. After perhaps 10 to 20 minutes of sitting still and quiet, we will dismiss some children to the van, usually one by one, with a last-minute instruction (buckle a child into a car seat, pack the diaper bag, pour Mom's coffee, etc.).

Such practice is good for any kind of church service or teaching atmosphere. Children will build good character and respect for parents and teachers. Sitting still and quiet for church is practical for our worshiping together, but it is also practical for the child who goes to Sunday school. The unruly child is a nightmare that makes a Sunday school teacher shudder. We assure you, your teachers will praise you for how well your children behave when you practice proper behavior at home on Sunday mornings.

Our kids enter church with a complete understanding of how they are expected to behave. There is no question. Worship is uninterrupted and quite pleasant. We've been practicing church every Sunday for about 10 years now, and Sunday morning is "restful" as it should be.

The Supermarket

We've all witnessed miserable mothers rolling their circus wagons down the isles of a supermarket. For instance, Mom carries her one son in the store with the honest prayer that he will behave (though nothing was done to prepare her son for *how* to behave). The first dispute begins with the choice of cart: her son wants the cool cart with the steering wheel. Because there aren't any available, Mom says no, her son cries, so she carries him back out to the parking lot till they find a cool cart in one of the stalls. Her son's contentment lasts till Aisle 1 when he discovers balancing on the moving cart is much more enjoyable than make-believe driving. Because Junior is ignoring his mother's numerous commands to sit down, Mom pushes him in place (a not-so-easy task) and buckles him in. This leads to approximately 5 or 6 aisles of wailing. Mom is so intent on finishing that she skips half her list and heads to the checkout. Junior remarkably becomes quiet. The checkout lady asks, "Are you going to pay for that?" Mom sees the candy bar (within reach from the cart) in the boy's hands. "Absolutely not!"

frustrated Mom says. More wailing resumes as the rest of the groceries run through the line. Junior starts to hit Mommy; Mommy slaps Junior on the hand; Junior cries and hits Mommy again; Mommy sends candy through the scanner, Mommy yells at the child, "*Fine*, you little brat, here's your candy. Now stop crying or you're going to get a spanking!" He stops crying, the checkout lady quickly runs the last items through, and the lady behind Mom is calling Social Services on her cell phone.

Meanwhile, Wendy Jeub has eleven of her 13 children with her—five of whom are under six-years-old—in a neighboring aisle. She has her shopping completed in two carts. She has said *no* to several requests for goodies and has given her final command, "Stop asking for things, please." The older children pull out their wallets and purses and buy their own goodies, and the younger kids look forward to politely asking them to share. Shopping is a pleasurable experience for Wendy and her children. *How does she do it*?

Different from the previous practice, there is more involved here than simply sitting still and quiet. Children in a supermarket need to understand the ever-so-important word *no*. We have heard modern psychologists make the incredibly weak argument that because *no* is a negative word, it should be said as seldom as possible. We think this is ridiculous. *No* is a *good* word whose meaning should be learned by all children. This is the trial of the Supermarket Mom: expecting the child to accept *no* for an answer with contentment and gratitude.

Even our toddlers learn the meaning of *no.* When sitting in our lap with untouchable items in front of him or her, we will use the opportunity to teach the meaning of *no.* For example, at dinner a 12-month-old may sit in our lap while Dad finishes supper. This toddler is very capable of grabbing Dad's plate and pulling his entire dinner onto the floor. This is a great opportunity to practice proper behavior. Dad, with a firm "no," will tell the toddler to not grab his plate. He quickly understands "no" as a firm direction to proper behavior, and he complies. When the toddler is taught to resist his temptation to grab everything in his range, dinnertime becomes much more enjoyable and manageable. Dad enjoys dinner and baby enjoys sitting on Dad's lap.

Older children (ages 2-6) may need a more practical lesson. Place a desirable object—a toy or some candy—in an opportune place for the child to see (at eye-level, much like the supermarket marketers do to our vulnerable little children). Placing the temptation of the reward in front of the child allows the child the opportunity to overcome his inclinations. Mom can firmly reinforce "no" with reasonable conditions. "No, this candy is for after lunch," or "No, you may play with this toy after you put away your other toys." If tantrums follow, discipline is needed. However, placing these practice sessions in front of the children will keep the need for discipline to a minimum. Once the child understands and accepts Mommy's "no" for an answer, going to the supermarket (or anywhere for that matter) becomes an enjoyable experience for both child and Mommy.

Going to Bed

The idea of practicing behavior can be applied to virtually any area of parenting you find frustrating. Several years ago, getting the kids to bed was chaos. We would collectively say our prayers, give kisses, and send the kids to bed. Our children followed this routine with numerous drinks of water, complaints of hunger, long bathroom visits, begs to read a book, whines of scary shadows, etc., etc. Threats of spankings seemed to draw the line in the sand, but it didn't make going to bed an enjoyable experience. The kids would push and push until that magic threat of corporal punishment. They weren't contently going to bed as they should, and Mom and Dad weren't enjoying the experience anymore than they were.

One *afternoon* (notice practicing doesn't happen when the behavior is required) we "practiced" going to bed. We went through a practice prayer time on the sofas. When we said, "Go to bed," we then made it a game as to who could get into bed under their covers first. We did this only once that afternoon. Guess what happened when they were told to go to bed that evening: *they went to bed.* They were happy about it, and Mom and Dad got to enjoy their last hour alone to wind down the day.

Our nightly routine hasn't changed much since. The kids are told to get dressed for bed and return to the living room sofas for prayers. We have more children now than we had several years ago when we started this routine. Chris starts the prayer time with a short prayer of thanksgiving and petition, to which we move down from the oldest child to the youngest (at least the youngest who can utter a prayer). Wendy is the last to pray. We then, together in unison, pray the following:

"God bless Mommy, Daddy, Alicia, Alissa, Cynthia, Lydia, Isaiah, Micah, Noah, Tabitha, Keilah, Hannah, Josiah, Havilah, Joshua, and Isaak."

We practice this most every night. Not only do we typically get a good night sleep, our household is at peace at the end of the day.

Practice Makes (Almost) Perfect

These three examples—sitting in church, shopping at the supermarket, and going to bed—are common experiences for virtually every family blessed with children. Practice doesn't make perfect children. Perfect obedience and perfect behavior is not attainable by us, let alone our children. There will be times of frustration even when you are trying to find creative ways to teach good behavior. We want to encourage you in this: *train up a child in the way he should go, and when he is old, he will not depart from it* (Proverbs 22:6). This is a promise to you as parents, so don't give up because of frustration. Quite the contrary: respond to your frustration with creative parenting solutions that build an atmosphere of learning and love.

Chapter 9

Building Relationships

When we see a family full of love—a family where love is truly in the house—we see a family that cares about each other. Family members that care about each other are the strongest of families. Small and large alike, families that have love in the house are families that care about building relationships.

Because they are more difficult to manage, large families tend to gravitate toward activities that bring them together rather than push them apart. Parents with a few kids are able to juggle complex schedules involving school activities, youth group, church, community, etc. We have *six times* more children than the average family. If we were to maintain half the schedule of some small families we know, we would not only drive ourselves to exhaustion but we would hardly see each other!

Social Similarities in Large Families

Large families have a lot of schedules to juggle. It is not uncommon to see families our size consolidate activities that are often separated by age group. When TLC set out to find three large families, the only criterion was having at least 12 natural born kids. It wasn't until later that they discovered several unique similarities with all three families.

First, all three families home school their children. Today home schooling is, for the most part, accepted as a healthy alternative to traditional education. We can't tell you how pleased we are with the relationships we've built with our children through our daily education. Wendy does most of the schooling, but Chris brings the older kids into his office twice a week to do lessons. While education is definitely high on the list of reasons we home school, the simple fact that we build stronger bonds with our children is even higher.

We can only imagine the headaches we would have to endure if we sent our kids to a traditional school. All of our children would have different teachers whom we would need to communicate with regularly. Each child would be in a separate grade. Homework would be assigned according to grade level rather than skill level. We know parents of a few children who look at our life of 13 kids and ask, "How do you do it?" We sometimes look back at them—their few kids, their school, their extracurricular and social lives, activity upon activity—and reply, "How do *you* do it?" It makes perfect sense to us that we, as parents of 13 children, would choose home education.

All three families involved in "Kids by the Dozen" not only choose home education as their method of educating their children, but we did so back in the days when it was not socially accepted. The Arndts, whose oldest children are in their 20s, have home schooled them all. The Heppners built a successful book distribution business for twenty years selling curriculum and resources for home school families across the upper Midwest and parts of Canada. We, too, built a ministry that caters to the home school debate league, the National Christian Forensics and Communications Association, the country's only nationally recognized home school extracurricular activity. We three families are not just home schooling; we have been home school advocates from the start of the home school movement. For the Jeub family, we started home schooling largely because of the relationship-building nature of the educational choice.

Another similarity has to do with church: All three families are involved in home church settings. Rick Arndt pastors his own church of a handful of families, and we get together with fewer than seven families every Sunday. The Heppners typically worship with a few family friends. Personally (not speaking for the Arndts or Heppners), we aren't opposed to traditional church formats, but we have found traditional settings difficult to work our family into. While ushering in and ushering out of church is what most families participate in week in and week out, we desire a much more casual, relational service, one where we can hang out for brunch and talk about the sermon or simply about what's going on in each family's life. We—and the other two families—enjoy the deep relationships of a smaller church.

You can see that the three families of the "Kids by the Dozen" miniseries have several similarities. There are more! All three fathers are self-employed, and they all have do-it-yourself tendencies. Both the Heppners and the Arndts built their own homes, and we have plans to do so in a few years. The Heppners and we both converted school busses into RVs. The Arndts currently have a local radio show on parenting, the Heppners continue to speak at home school conferences, and we write curriculum every year for the debate league.

This makes sense: large families tend to resist conformity and replace it with social activities that include large numbers of people. We value family relationships just like any parent should, and we as parents of many children create social environments that strengthen these relationships. Through our schooling, employment choices, church relationships, and social activities, we create environments that bring us together, and we avoid the activities that drive us apart.

Sibling Relationships

TIME magazine made a significant splash with an article about sibling influence. We chuckled at the title, "The New Science of Siblings," as if it were something *new.* The article validates much of what we have believed for a long time. We believe most parents are guilty of thinking that *parental* influence on a child is the most significant influence in that child's life. However, some studies are showing that a more influential dynamic in a child's life can be his or her siblings. The article is subtitled, "Your parents raised you; your spouse lives with you; but it's your brothers and sisters who really shaped you."

> From the time they are born, our brothers and sisters are our collaborators and co-conspirators, our role models and cautionary tales. They are our scolds, protectors, goads, tormentors, playmates, counselors, sources of envy, objects of pride. They teach us how to resolve conflicts and how not to; how to conduct friendships and when to walk away from them. Sisters teach brothers about the mysteries of girls; brothers teach sisters about the puzzle of boys. Our spouses arrive comparatively late in our lives; our parents eventually leave us. Our siblings may be the only people we'll ever know who truly qualify as partners for life. "Siblings," says family sociologist Katherine Conger of the University of California, Davis, "are with us for the whole journey.[11]

Parents often plan their family size based on how many kids *they* can handle. As parents, perhaps we fail to consider the healthy dynamics of siblings. TIME confesses that "the first thing that strikes contemporary researchers when they study siblings is the sheer quantity of time the kids spend in one another's presence and the power that has to teach them social skills." Parents who have strong—or weak—sibling connections can testify to the power of sibling relationships. There is a very natural wonder that happens between brothers and sisters. Research centers are…

> "…looking at ways brothers and sisters steer one another into—or away from—risky behavior; how they form a protective buffer against family upheaval; how they educate one another about the opposite sex; how all siblings compete

> for family recognition and come to terms—or blows—over such impossibly charged issues as parental favoritism."

We both can testify to this in our own lives growing up. I (Chris) grew up with three sisters, and their relationship with each other is incredibly close, and they each had a profound influence on my life. Though I had wonderful parents, Becky, Katy and Heidi had likely more to do with the shaping of my personality and character.

I (Wendy) come from an alcoholic family (though my mother, thankfully, has found sobriety in the past few years). I was raised with five siblings. Reflecting on my childhood, I believe it was the strong sibling bonds of the six kids that kept me resilient to the pressures of my difficult circumstances. I recently took a trip to Wisconsin and Minnesota to visit family, and the most memorable of visits were those with my sisters Heather, Paula and Debbi, and our visit to my brother, Tod, who was caring for my mother. It stands without doubt that my family is a strong unit today primarily because of the strong sibling bonds that have galvanized over the years.

The dynamic relationships between our children are incredible. Alicia and Alissa, our two oldest who are adults on their own, have a unique bond between them that, in some ways, is stronger than the bonds they have with us. When we visit for holidays and backyard barbeques, the family dynamics when they are together are energized compared to when they are apart. The same is with the 11 at home. When they are alone or apart from each other, the intensity of the relationships goes down a notch. Sure, with more people comes more quarrels and turmoil, but we wouldn't trade it for anything. The TIME article validates this, "As much as all the fighting can set parents' hair on end, there's a lot of learning going on too, specifically about how conflicts, once begun, can be settled." The article concludes, "Siblings, by any measure, are one of nature's better brainstorms."

We'd say that there is more than just nature involved in the blessing of siblings. Children are a heritage of the Lord's. Nevertheless, the TIME article opens another angle to our understanding—and backs it up with scientific proof—of the blessings of children. Not only are they blessings to the parents, but to one other.

Loving Relationships

We have not been perfect parents any more than our children have been perfect kids. The longer we parent and the more children we have, the more we are convinced that loving one another is the most important thing we need to master in life. Some argue that having so many children weakens our ability to love them all, but we disagree. There is a multiplying phenomenon that occurs in large families where there is strength in numbers and a compounding of love.

As already mentioned, I (Wendy) came from a broken family. However, I never used this as an excuse for making poor choices as a parent myself. We all have choices to make, and choosing to love your children is the greatest of all choices. Failing to consciously make the choice to love can, unfortunately, hinder your relationship with your children.

A couple years ago I began to view my children in a unique way. I envisioned them with a sign around their neck that read, "I don't know that you love me." This is the truth: they don't know for sure. It is very easy for parents to take for granted that their children know their love for them. We do dishes, fold laundry, tuck them in at night, and work our tails off for them; naturally, we *assume* they know our love for them, but they don't. My parenting changed for the better when I recognized that I needed to verbally show my love for my children.

I have shown this in both subtle and direct ways. Standing in the kitchen making dinner, I'll blurt out, "Cynthia, I want you to know that I really, really love you." When my 5-year-old brings me a book to read to her, I'll say, "Hannah, if I didn't have a Hannah just like you, I would *want* a Hannah just like you." I say things like this constantly. As I say these words of affirmation of my love for them, I transform my thinking, I believe them to be true, and my children grow to believe the same.

I also see my kids—especially when they grow into teenagers—each with an emotional cup. He or she brings me the cup daily as if to say, "Please fill my cup today, Mom." This is shown by bringing a book to read, playing a game, help with schoolwork, etc. If I don't pour my love into the cup, the child will eventually turn away and seek other avenues for the love for which they hope. Parents should not give up filling their children's cups with love.

So far in this book we have attempted to encourage you to allow God to bless your family life. Overcoming fears, being creative, embracing freedom, practicing proper behavior, developing relationships—these are all good and worthy objectives parents should have. The practical applications in this book all boil down to one main objective, a *most important* objective. This is *love*, a virtue too often underrated in busy families. We are guilty of missing the mark on loving relationships in the past. Through our trials—which we share in the remaining chapters—we have come to the firm conclusion that Love in the House is the greatest of goals.

Chapter 10

What Went Wrong?

We used to think that love was overrated. A moral sense of right and wrong was much more important than "warm and fuzzy" feelings like love. While love no doubt made for good poetry, the truth *behind* love, not love itself, was the marrow of life.

Describing our early years together may help you understand why we used to think this way. I (Chris) became an avid student of the Bible after my enthusiastic conversion to Christianity at age 17. I (Wendy) became a Christian as a child but didn't start a dedicated life to Christ until I was mentored in a Bible-believing church as a single mom. We were married 10 months after we met, and we were naturally drawn to evangelical churches, particularly ones that helped refine our convictions about the importance of family. We pursued holiness with diligence.

Once again, that's how we *used* to think.

Have we entirely abandoned our old way of life? Not necessarily, and the preceding chapters are evidence of that. However, in our quest for holiness, we failed at *loving our children above all*. We strove for perfection in our spiritual walk, only to be left with an emptiness that, as we'll show later, crippled our family. What we dismissed as mere window dressing (i.e. love) was actually the entire panorama outside. It would have been much easier to fill this book with talk about shopping lists, folding laundry, and other pragmatic strategies for making a large family work. We now believe that love is the most important character quality for families to master. Without it, life is a dank, empty room—cut off completely from the glories of the world outside.

Our family recently endured a very challenging time in our lives—one that, thankfully, brought us to a heightened understanding of how important love really is. This chapter reveals an ugly failure in our parenting history: A lack of love. We have 13 kids, some of whom were raised in a home that—while certainly not absent of love—placed a greater emphasis on performance and legalism. Yet we have learned from this mistake, and it is our hope that in sharing our story, we can help other families avoid learning this lesson the hard way.

Our Case Study

Our heartbreaking lesson in love revolved around our oldest daughter, Alicia, whose story was briefly highlighted in our "Kids by the Dozen" episode.[12] When Alicia graduated from high school, she made plans to attend a local community college for a year before moving east to study at a conservative Christian university. Being the socialite of the family, she got a job at a dental office (a very nice job for an 18-year-old) to help pay for tuition, her car and the necessities of life. Alicia always had an innate sense of responsibility, so she also spent time housesitting for some family friends. Alicia attended church with us regularly while starting to build a life for herself.

Little did we know, but Alicia was living a double life. She secretly had no plans to continue her education beyond the community college. Instead of visiting coffee shops to study, she frequented dance clubs. She continued to attend prayer meetings and youth gatherings, but, while telling us she was going out with Christian friends afterwards, she would head off to parties instead (with some of the same kids who were at the youth gatherings). She even hosted some of these parties at the home where she was housesitting.

We had no idea this was going on until one of Alicia's friends told her mom who, in turn, told us. For the next several weeks (by this time Alicia was 19), we sought our pastor's counsel and tried diligently to reason with our daughter. Family friends spent hours talking with Alicia about the destructiveness of her behavior. We even flew her to Minnesota to spend time at the same religious retreat we both experienced when we were her age.

In the end, Alicia chose to forsake her family and her faith. Her new lifestyle included promiscuity, alcohol, swearing, smoking and who knows what else. It was as if Alicia made mental note of everything her parents despised, and then ran after it. As if that wasn't enough, Alicia's newfound attitude was nearly unbearable. She lied to the point that we couldn't trust anything she said; she fought with us about the most trivial things; she was intentionally cruel to her 17-year-old sister; and she attempted to emotionally manipulate her younger siblings whenever there was an argument or conflict.

Our home was a wreck, to the point that the entire family suffered from the turmoil. The house turned into a mess, the kids ran wild, and Mom and Dad spent countless hours agonizing over their lost child. We came to the stark conclusion that our daughter no longer wanted to be around us, and we couldn't emotionally afford to keep her at home against her will. We asked her to move out, and she gladly agreed.

We didn't sever our relationship with Alicia right away. It took several months before we finally cut off all communication. Even though she was free at last from her parent's rule, she continued to grow in anger and resentment. Her relationship with her parents was in shambles, but Alicia would still stop in and visit her siblings. We were naturally concerned for the negative influence she might have on the other children, so we insisted that she work with us on our relationship. But this only led to more quarrels and more separation and, over time, to virtually no contact at all.

This took place nearly three years prior to our experience with TLC, and Alicia hadn't seen her brothers and sisters since that final split occurred. We made a few attempts to meet with her, but they usually ended in bitter argument. When our twins were born in October 2005, Alicia tried to reach out with what appeared to be sincere compassion and a desire to reconcile, but we were hesitant to respond in kind. We traded e-mails over several months, but nothing seemed to work. During our eight-day stint with the TLC crew, we treated Alicia simply as an adult child who didn't care to be around the family, and the production company was fine with that.

We were hesitant to share this part of our story with TLC—and, ultimately, with the world—for three reasons. First, we did not want to embarrass Alicia. We didn't want people to express judgment that would likely drive her even further away from her family. Second, we weren't so keen on being judged ourselves! The producers and editors could have easily manipulated the footage to show how we, as parents, were overly strict and legalistic.[13] Third, we didn't yet know the end of the story. When the camera crew arrived, Alicia was still estranged from the family. There were no plans for reconciliation or any sort of third-party mediation. Our relationship was at a stalemate, and it didn't appear to be changing anytime soon.

What Went Wrong?

We have quite a few friends who knew of our struggles with Alicia and tried to help us make sense of the situation. We never attempted to cover up our estrangement, but this didn't stop observers from offering their own assessments. We welcomed input from our friends.

Alicia was always intelligent. In fact, she made it to nationals in the National Christian Forensics and Communication Association by delivering an oratory speech *on purity.* One of the most therapeutic times for us was going through Alicia's belongings after she left: Bible study notes, worldview academy journals, courtship and betrothal articles highlighted and underlined by our daughter. These were the things she didn't want any longer. Alicia certainly received an adequate—in fact, we'd proudly say *excellent*—education on proper and ladylike behavior. Some of our friends who knew Alicia well could hardly believe that she turned to a promiscuous lifestyle.

In fact, some of our friends responded by challenging us directly. One couple (with eight children of their own) couldn't stop asking *what we did wrong.* Some approached Alicia in search of an explanation. Could it be that her rebellion was due to the fact that she attended public school from kindergarten through second grade? Was she abused at a young age? Perhaps Alicia just got in with the wrong crowd. When confronted, Alicia denied any external causes for her rebellion. In fact, the very idea that her decisions were not her own made her angry. "I'm choosing this because it is *what I want!*" she insisted.

Some people accused us of being too strict. Alicia, perhaps, was simply rebelling against all our rules. We never really believed this. We're still strict; though now we make sure our strictness is bathed in love. We see nothing wrong with setting relational and spiritual boundaries. Parents must teach children right from wrong. We're of the opinion that too many parents *aren't strict enough*, that allowing kids too much freedom is a very bad idea. Besides, Alicia had no shortage of freedom and opportunity as an adult child, so much so that she was able to maintain a double life. The people who said we were too strict simply didn't know us well enough to see how reasonable we really were.

Sin is sin, others said, and we are all susceptible to sin. When tempted, Alicia simply fell. It's true that we know other families whose kids have "fallen," but they didn't result in the same level of devastation. Shortly before we learned of Alicia's deception, one friend of ours, a pastor, found out that his daughter had gotten pregnant while attending Bible college. The daughter quickly repented, however, and today she is happily married and united with her parents. Another friend just last year got word that his son, the oldest son of nine children, had impregnated his girlfriend. While his future plans for college and career faded away, the young man married his girlfriend and is today making the best of their life. In short, both these ugly situations were mended and the families reconciled. So why was our relationship with Alicia so cold for so long?

Still others judged us for *not being strict enough*. We frequent very conservative circles. Some of our friends won't allow their girls to wear pants or their boys to wear shorts, nor will they allow them to watch PG-13 movies or even TV. In fact, we know full well that some of our friends looked at our perceived "permissiveness" with Alicia as reasons for her fall, even *after* Alicia was a legal adult. Sure, Alicia often argued with us about her clothes, curfew and the like. And as all parents do, we tried to pick our battles as wisely as we could.

Still, we hoped for the best with Alicia and allowed her the freedom to choose as she saw fit, only to the extent it didn't harm the other children. We don't believe our leniency in some areas was the cause for her rebellion.

Our friends spent countless hours trying to discern a reason for Alicia's decisions, but most were left scratching their heads along with us. Alicia came from *a good family*, we concluded, one that embraced faith and good moral standing. We tried to obey God in all our choices and worked hard to raise our children according to the righteousness and calling of God. We simply could not figure out *what went wrong*.

Chapter 11

Our Lesson in Love

Like many Christians, we read the Bible daily and make ourselves students of Scripture. We believe that the Bible is literally the Word of God. We take great care in making sure we *get it right* in interpreting and living out what the Bible teaches.

This is why we now think ourselves such fools for missing the profundity of love as it is laid out in the New Testament. Jesus Christ—whom we profess to be the Lord of our life—took great care in making sure His disciples knew that *everything* He did was born out of love. John 3:16, probably the best-known verse among evangelicals, says: "God so *loved* the world that He gave His only son." Our wedding ceremony was replete with talk about love—including a word-for-word reading of 1 Corinthians 13 (also known as "the love chapter")—yet we still somehow considered it secondary to our performance and our parenting. The fourth chapter of 1 John even states it twice: *God is love*. How could we miss God's many reminders that love is *the most important virtue?*

Perhaps you don't agree that it is the *most* important. Here is a list of verses—and there are plenty more throughout Scripture—that illustrate how important love is in life, let alone parenting:

- "Whoever does not love does not know God, because God is love" (1 John 4:8).
- "We know that we all possess knowledge. Knowledge puffs up, but love builds up" (1 Corinthians 8:1).
- "Yet I hold this against you: You have forsaken your first love" (Revelations 2:4).
- "Now that you have purified yourselves by obeying the truth so that you have sincere love for your brothers, love one another deeply, from the heart" (1 Peter 1:22).
- "This is how we know what love is: Jesus Christ laid down his life for us. And we ought to lay down our lives for our brothers" (1 John 1:13).

Consider the many stories in Scripture that elevate love to the highest level. When questioned about the greatest commandment, Jesus had a ready answer: *Love* the Lord God and *love* your neighbor. "All the Law of the Prophets," He said, "hang on these two commandments" (Matthew 22:40, in context v. 34-40). In fact, the Gospel of John tells of Jesus creating a new commandment: "Love one another. As I have loved you, so you must love one another" (John 13:34).

Jesus dined with tax-collectors, befriended prostitutes, and stood between the stone-throwers and those accused (and likely guilty) of sin. Did this look like our life? The Jeubs sought out family-friendly churches, attended home school conferences and worked diligently to keep our children free from sinful lifestyles. Yet the verse from John continues: "By this all men will know that you are my disciples, if you love one another" (John 13:35). Was Jesus really reflected in our family's feeble attempts at perfection?

Love is not just one of many virtues; it is *the most important* virtue, the "most excellent way" (1 Corinthians 12:31). If you are part of a church that regularly meditates on God's love and the Greatest Commandment, you are truly blessed. Read your church's bulletin and see what the activities center around. Bible memorization, how to be good parents, how wives should submit to their husbands, how to be "manly men," the influence of modern culture, the importance of voting, how to manage money, etc. These are good things, sure, but does your church focus *first* on loving God and loving one another?

We thought we did everything right with Alicia. In fact, we *were preached* that if parents parented *correctly,* they would surely produce *good kids.* We were behaviorists to a T. Like with Pavlov's dog, if you parented the right way (e.g. consistent discipline, devotions, spanking, training, etc.), you could simply ring a bell and good kids would come running. Today, we're no longer parents who stubbornly proclaim, "We did everything right, therefore we're not to blame!" Oh no. We are down on our knees asking God *and Alicia* to forgive us for missing the most important thing of all: *love.*

Separations in Our Lives

We never intended to tell the world about our private conflict. The camera crew was in the last couple days of filming when we first explained our estrangement from our oldest daughter. The onsite producer was able to meet Alicia the day before he flew back to New York, where he shared with the executive producer and the editors the story of our prodigal child. (They confessed to us later that they had to look up "prodigal" in a dictionary and locate a Bible to understand what we meant by the term.) The producers agreed to fly out another camera crew for two days of additional interviews. This new footage became the final segment of our "Kids by the Dozen" episode.

We decided to share this part of our story because we know there are countless other families experiencing similar pain and disappointment. We hoped that our transparency could help heal others' broken relationships, but this left us vulnerable to some very pointed questions from the camera crew. The producer asked questions like, "You talk so much about love, but you don't let your oldest daughter come to your Birthday Bash?" or "You were rebellious when you were younger; why can't you overlook Alicia's rebellion?" Alicia had become pregnant and had a child in the last three years of our separation, so this begged the question to Wendy, "Why aren't you more sympathetic to Alicia's situation?" All this while the cameras rolled.

The onsite producer was just doing his job, and it was our job to explain ourselves. We wish we could say we had this all figured out before the cameras arrived to capture our responses, but we didn't. We were hoping to fix a broken relationship with our oldest daughter; we didn't know the way home; we didn't have the answers. The interview became more uncomfortable as we tried to explain our decision to keep Alicia away from the other children—so uncomfortable, in fact, that we began to regret the whole idea. Nevertheless, we did our best to explain ourselves.

Most of our answers ended up on the editing-room floor. We referenced the story of the prodigal son (Luke 15:11-32) to explain how we viewed ourselves as parents "in waiting" for Alicia to return to her family with a repentant heart. We explained how Alicia, being the oldest, had a great amount of influence—albeit *negative* influence—on her younger siblings. Alicia, unfortunately, posed a genuine threat to our other children. We explained how difficult it was—without being too specific—to believe anything Alicia said, since so much of her recent past consisted of double-talk and deception.

The editors back east had their own struggles understanding our relationship with our daughter. I (Chris) received a frustrated phone call from one of the studio editors who couldn't see what "the story" was. He needed details in order to edit the segment. I attempted to explain to him that the details of the conflict were not that important—that more parents would identify with this prodigal story if we actually left the details out. The editor wasn't satisfied with my explanation. "What did Alicia do that was so bad?" he wanted to know. "That's not what is important," I replied. Thus went an hour-long telephone conversation.

"Look," I finally said, growing agitated at where this was heading, "I know you want more than ever for Alicia and her parents to reconcile, right?" The editor agreed. "Aren't their separations in your life?" He admitted this was indeed the case. I continued: "I would like nothing more than for you to reconcile with this person, but it isn't quite that simple, is it?"

The editor had to agree. He at last saw the universality in the story, and he was now ready to tackle the footage captured in those two days. That same footage could have easily resulted in a documentary that built two cases (Alicia's and ours) and then let the world judge who was right and who was wrong. That's what most modern reality television does, and that's what the editor was used to creating. To him, our family's story was just another tale of separation and estrangement, yet I wanted him to understand that millions of people could identify with our situation. We weren't able to articulate it then—and neither could the producers or the editors—but we were getting close to a truth that would literally transform our family.

Chapter 12

How Love Can Lead

Three years ago, when we first learned of our oldest daughter's rebellion, we would dream of reconciliation that looked something like this: Alicia would return home with a broken heart and a ruined life. She would submit to our authority as parents, to which we would lovingly respond with open arms. We would throw a party much like the one the prodigal son's father threw for his son. Our steadfast love for our daughter would eventually win out and lead to a dramatic change in her behavior.

We now see that we had fallen for a lie that's been around for years. Since the beginning of history, mankind has been judging one another as if they were God. We believe such judgments are better exercised by God than us. People all over the world watched our episode on TLC and no doubt some cast a fair amount of judgment on our situation. Based on the e-mail we received through our website, some judged us as overbearing parents while others judged Alicia as an ungrateful rebel. Our story, however, was not that simple. Thankfully, we have a relationship with God that is overflowing with grace and understanding. God continues to work on us as parents and on Alicia as an adult, and this situation needed divine intervention.

Trouble was, all this judgment flying around created a binding scenario that left little room for God to heal our relationship. Friends and outsiders either judged us for being overly protective or judged Alicia for being rebellious. TLC was asking tough questions to help their viewers act as judges. Finally, we were judging Alicia for the choices she had made.

We began to see how wrong we were. Didn't Jesus Himself make this clear? "Do not judge, or you too will be judged" (Matthew 7:1, Luke 6:37). These words are commonly quoted by non-believers to show how Christians are hypocrites, which is why we never paid them much heed. However, this verse reminds us how tempting it is to condemn *others* for their sins. This kind of judgment is *man-made*, and man-made judgment often keeps people from loving relationships with God and each other. No one—not parents of large families nor prodigal children—appreciate being under the microscope of judgment. In fact, judgment tends to poison everything. The person being judged doesn't like it, and the person judging becomes a bitter crab. There is no reconciliation, no repentance, and no hope. *And no love*. Our notion that our approach would help Alicia one day conform to our judgment was a fantasy void of the kind of love God shows us.

Alicia's parents aren't perfect. We have many faults and weaknesses, but we can still be good parents because God labors in love with us. God doesn't look at us with disappointment and ridicule due to our failings; He reaches out His hand with a loving invitation to unite with Him for eternity.

This is the Good News from Romans 5:8: that Christ died for us (the ultimate testimony of love) while we were yet sinners (not after we had it all together). Conversion to Christianity is not a conclusion: It is a beginning. The prodigal son's father was not standing at the doorstep with his arms folded, tapping his foot in judgment. In fact, he didn't even give his son a chance to explain himself. He ran out to greet his son, wrapped his arms around him and accepted him *just as he was*. No condemnation, no penance, no list of rules to adhere to.

It wasn't till we realized how our judgment was lacking in love that we found the path to reconciliation. This was such a significant realization—so profound in our Christian growth—that we look back with deep regret at the broken relationships we have suffered through. In some cases, we were the instigators. We hear from many parents of large-families who are judged by their relatives and friends for having so many kids. We now realize that *we* have judged friends and relatives for their choice of *not* having kids. Is that any business of ours? No! Only God can judge the hearts of people, not us. Our duty is in loving God and loving others.

First Steps to Reconciliation

Taking this realization to Alicia made our knees tremble. I (Chris) scheduled two lunches with our daughter within a week's time. It had been nearly three years since I had made any serious attempt to reconcile. Sure enough, Alicia had no desire to repent of anything she didn't think was wrong, but for the first time, I felt free from judging her. The first lunch went beautifully. It was relaxing, a time to catch up on our lives, and a time of jokes and laughter. This was also my introduction to Alicia's son Isaak, my first and only grandson to date. I pulled out my camera and recorded some video that ended up in the conclusion of the TLC episode.

The second lunch was not all smiles. I confessed to Alicia my sin of judgment. "I am sorry," I said, "for raising you in the house of a Pharisee." I explained what a Pharisee was. "They were the teachers of the law who had all their religious ducks in a row, but they loved no one. When Jesus showed up with the claim that God is Love, it was the Pharisees who plotted to kill Him. Jesus reserved His harshest words for the Pharisees, while tax collectors, prostitutes and the fishermen of the day received tender words of love and compassion. Alicia, I am so sorry for judging you. I want to relearn how to love you if you will give me the chance."

The walls came crumbling down. Tears were shed right there at the table. Alicia—the one who had lost all interest in church or God—demonstrated a remarkable act of grace by forgiving her father. It was so easy to reconcile with her that all the fears of the past were wiped away. At that moment, love cast out fear.

Since that day, we have once again opened our lives to each other. Alicia is facing some hard consequences of her past behavior. Isaak's biological father is presently entitled to court-ordered visitation. Only 2 years old, Issak is emotionally distraught over the situation. Alicia has a restraining order against Isaak's father, but she continues to fight for custody. The ordeal is tearing Alicia apart.

In our old, pharisaical state of mind, we would have likely condemned Alicia for her mistakes. Didn't we teach her for 18 years to avoid such choices? Alicia went looking for trouble, and, boy, did she find it. Now she's learning life the hard way. "Don't come crying to us, Alicia, you're getting what you deserve." *Oh, Lord, how cruel we can be!*

Alicia *has* come crying to us, and we have enjoyed responding to her vulnerability with compassion. We don't need to judge her; she's already kicking herself enough for her past decisions. Because we have not condemned her, she has opened up to us about the complexities of her situation, and we, in turn, have been able to counsel her. We shudder to think of what our relationship would be like if we had met Alicia with condemnation. She would still be alone, struggling to make decisions, without the love and support of her parents.

We are relearning how to love.

Love in the House

Why is this lesson so significant? Because *everyone* faces separation at some point in life. People leave, people hate, people lash out—and they don't often enjoy a loving response. And it's not only rebellious youth that bring heartbreak. Divorce, abuse, crime, neighborhood squabbles, gossip—all are results of separation and, in reality, an absence of love. Furthermore, we all want to shake our fists at those who have done us wrong. The world we live in is plagued with separation from each other, and from God. Life on earth is hell without love to heal it.

We are relearning how to love Alicia, yes, but we are also relearning how to love all our children. Alissa, our second child, also grew up in a home of Pharisees, though she found comfort in conformity and obedience. The other kids are young enough that we've been able to undo much of the damage, but they have received sour teaching nonetheless. Everything we do today as parents—the church we attend, the activities we choose, how we correct and discipline—are now filtered through a lens of love. We will not attend churches that attempt to create a safe haven from "those sinners" in the world. We will not choose activities that breed self-centeredness or family division. We will not ridicule or shame our children into behaviors we desire. We can fail at almost anything as parents, but if we succeed in love, we have little to worry about.

This realization has been so life-shaking, so incredible, that we now say we have been *reborn*. Sure, we have been Christians for many years, but now we recognize the true power of Christ to transform the world. Jesus Christ came into the world to *save sinners* (that means *everybody*), and He told us exactly what to do. The Greatest Commandment is to love God and love each other. So simple, yet so easy to miss. Godly love is amazing, the kind of love that, when realized, can't help but create tears in your eyes and a lump in your throat. Such love is infinite; it overflows from those who show it and can fill a hole in the most dysfunctional heart.

When the love of Christ takes up residence in a home, worries about material needs seem insignificant. When love is in the house, there is freedom to be all you can be. When parents and children live in love, once common fears become silly, passing thoughts. We look forward to watching all our children grow. We look forward to what they will become with great anticipation, even if it means we have to endure a time of rebellion. We know we'll make it through, because God is love, and because He is alive and well in our home.

Appendix

Frequently Asked Questions

With a family our size, questions come from all sorts of people. We have an FAQ (Frequently Asked Questions) page on our website that we field questions from visitors. We welcome you to visit our family website at *www.jeubfamily.com* and post your question, if it is not answered here.

How do you handle fights between siblings?

Recognizing that sibling rivalry has been around since Cain and Abel can relieve much of the pressure. Kids will fight; they're wired that way (just don't let them kill each other!). The Jeub kids are no exception. However, we have applied some helpful rules in our home that help keep fights to a minimum.

1. Setting Tone. Mom and Dad set the tone in the family. You don't want it to be set by a bunch of fighting kids. Turn the TV sitcoms off because they typically make a joke about sibling rivalry. Starting the day off with devotions and discussions about how to get along with one another helps. When Mom and Dad are tempered, their children usually are too.

2. Routine. Fights typically start up when there is a bit of chaos going on in the home. When we (the parents) veer from our schedule, fights inevitably rise up. Instead, when the family routine is unfolding and kids are part of the events of the day, fights don't happen nearly as often.

3. The Fighting Rule. We don't have a rule that says, "No fighting." Kids need to learn how to handle conflicts with one another. Our rule is simple and works most of the time. *"If Mom and Dad need to get involved, both will get what they DON'T want."* This sometimes ends with unfair rulings (some fights are started by one ill-mannered kid), but they are the exception. If the kids, instead of going to Mom or Dad, choose to beat each other up in the other room (an abusive situation), we parents will consider Mom or Dad needing to get involved even when the kids don't come to us initially.

4. Individual Personalities. Some of our kids are sweet natures and seldom get into fights. Others are controlling or annoying. We try to focus on *behavior* rather than *personalities*. Focusing on personality usually leads to a subtle ridiculing of a particular child and a favoring of the "sweeter" ones. Love that annoying child, but work with him or her to correct unpleasant behavior.

5. Apologizing. When the kids offend another child, we "make" them apologize. Sure, their hearts may still be angry with their sibling, but we believe at least faking it is helpful. They inevitably grow to see the benefits of forgiveness and love. Our kids have grown up in an atmosphere where saying sorry is easily done and accepted. This apologizing isn't limited to the kids, either; Mom and Dad often apologize when our tempers get the best of us and we fail to be as "cool" as we should be.

How do you keep things quiet?

We do a number of things to keep the noise down in our house. One, whenever too many kids are talking or shouting over one another, I (Wendy) will yell "Tower!" and the kids reply in unison, "Babel!" Then silence is expected. I then get the chance to talk and everyone listens.

We also have daily quiet time where the children are required to find something to do by themselves that is quiet. This can include reading, doing homework, playing a game, or working on a project. This is usually the time I take advantage of to take a nap!

A general rule that we try to keep is avoiding talking over other people. When eating a meal together, we practice this often. This teaches the kids to be considerate of others and listen or join in conversation. This is challenging for little kids, but not impossible.

How do you celebrate birthdays?

We have probably the most creative solution for birthdays imaginable. Our Jeub Birthday Bash was featured on TLC. We gather our friends and family together once a year for a "jeubilee" where we have games, a pinata, food, fellowship and much more.

On the kids' real birthdays, we have our simple traditions. We serve the child breakfast in bed. This is where siblings shower the birthday boy or girl with presents. We cook their favorite meal for dinner. We end their birthday with cake and sing happy birthday to them. Their individual birthdays are low key, and we let loose at the yearly Birthday Bash.

How do you deal with all the toys?

We keep all the toys in large bins. We don't have many shelves or a play room. When the kids get too many toys to manage, we start throwing the broken ones out or consider getting rid of the old, less interesting toys altogether. We go through toys fast; our kids wear them out.

Truth be known, we don't have as many toys as people think we do. We gear our lives to group games and toys that can be shared. The kids don't have many toys that are theirs alone.

What recipes do you enjoy?

We are planning to publish a cookbook that is specially designed for frugal families. For now, here is a list of common meals and an explanation of how they are easily expandable (i.e. we can make a lot of it) and how they are inexpensive to make.

1. Marinated Pork Ribs. We typically find pork ribs on sale at our local supermarket. We buy up a bunch when they drop below $1 per pound. We marinate them and grill them. We all love pork ribs served with mashed potatoes.

2. Crock pot meals. Mom has a knack for mixing up basics such as a can of soup, rice/potatoes, and some meat. These are nice when we are on the go for the day, because we can come home to a meal that has been cooking without supervision. Popular varieties are Tater Tot Hotdish, Chicken n' Rice and Elk n' Potato Layers.

3. Italian Pasta. With the help of a Sam's Club size can of tomato sauce, we can easily feed our family. We spice and stretch the sauce with hamburger or elk, then serve it over spaghetti, macaroni, or egg noodles. We often substitute hamburger with shredded zucchini that makes it stretch the penny.

4. Tacos. We buy large packages of tortillas and corn chips. Many hands in the kitchen are needed to help shred cheese and chop our lettuce, tomatoes, and olives. With beans, hamburger, and sour cream, everyone designs their own burrito. Another favorite is taco plate or salad, which combines all ingredients to be served over chips.

5. Soups and Salads are a snap when simple things are on hand. Egg, tuna, and chicken salads can be made into sandwiches or sides by adding pasta or bread. Soups are common and fun because they can consist of any dried or canned veggie simmered for awhile.

6. Meat pies are old fashioned and don't require many side dishes. After it has pressure cooked, any beef, elk, pork, or chicken can be chopped into a crust with gravy and vegetables.

7. Rolling Meals. A good tip to help stretch meals is to roll them into each other. Start with Spaghetti one day, and use the leftover sauce as a base for chili the next. Any chicken n' rice can be spiced up into an Asian meal the next evening with soy sauce.

8. Pizza. Another favorite is Pizza. Many crusts work well if they are rolled out and topped with leftover Spaghetti sauce and Mozzarella cheese. Add any topping you like from pepperoni and sausage to pineapple and onions.

9. Breakfast can be difficult on rushed mornings. We have come to avoid breakfast cereal due to the amount of sugar and air. Oatmeal is far more nutritious and it is warm and filling. Donuts and cake are not to be pushed away in our house. After all, they contain equal if not more nutrients than most cereals, and they are easy to serve. On the weekends, we make what we call a "Big Breakfast" consisting of meat, eggs, toast, and potatoes.

10. Bread. I (Wendy) find myself looking for extra time to make fresh biscuits or bun for a meal. Experimenting with different recipes will help, and chilling the dough ahead of time is also helpful.

What do you do in your home school?

We have been home schooling for 15 years, and we have become quite certain that there is no silver bullet in home schooling. Every school is unique, and that is what home schooling should be. Be creative to come up with solutions that work for you and your family. We like to share what works best for us, but when we see families try to copy us exactly, it never works out nicely. Please, be creative and enjoy the freedom in your home school!

Chris is the English teacher. He brings Lydia, Isaiah, Micah, Noah and Tabitha to the office twice a week for grammar, handwriting, reading and writing. Cynthia and I keep Keilah, Hannah and Josiah to do basic reading. On the days when I have all of them, we read literature and tie unit studies to them. We also enjoy science projects. Chris brings Cynthia, Lydia and Isaiah to debate club on Thursday nights. We study for AWANA which we attend weekly as an entire family. We attend PE+ (a phys. ed. class) every week.

How do you cook for such a large family?

I (Wendy) wish we had industrial size everything, but we don't. We have a standard stove and a modest-sized kitchen. We do have extra large novelty items like a 20-qt. soup kettle, an electric roaster that can easily fit a 20-lb turkey, a Kitchen Aid, two refrigerators and a 15-cubic foot chest freezer.

Chris and I used to do *Once a Month Cooking*. We did it for 7 years straight, but lost interest when we moved to Colorado (no particular reason why; we still highly recommend it). Even so, we frequently cook several servings at once and freeze the extra. This cuts down on the need to cook afresh everyday. It also disciplines me and helps keep my shopping costs down.

I have three meals that I almost always cook during the week: tacos, soup and chili. This knocks out nearly half the week, they are inexpensive meals, and I can always count on them. The other four days I (or more often my oldest daughter at home, Cynthia) can be a little more creative. Nevertheless, whatever we eat, cost efficiency is always our top goal.

How do you keep a clean house?

Clean house? To be honest, a dozen kids make big messes very quickly. However, we believe that a dozen kids can clean the house just as fast. Here's what we do to utilize the man power at the Jeub home.

"Two-minute clean ups" are quite popular around here. The parent will set the timer for two minutes and start it with a "go!" Kids will run everywhere trying to find things to put away. The parent simply monitors how fast and efficient everyone is. When the two minutes are up, the kids line up and wait for the parent to call off who the fastest kid was. The winner gets to sit out for the next two minutes. This game motivates everyone to move fast, and cleaning a disaster of a house can sometimes take less than 10 minutes.

What do you drive?

We have graduated to larger and larger vehicles over the years. Our family is so big, even a 15-passenger van seems crowded. This is what we drive: a 15-passenger van. (Chris has a smaller Ford Explorer for work.) We like to have the back seat out for storage, allowing us the ability to haul 11 people around. We place the farthest seat in the back, sacrificing the storage, to get us all in the van for church.

This makes a bus most comfortable. When we travel, it is often in our 1984 GMC 65-passenger school bus. We converted it three years ago into a registered and totally legit RV. Traveling around in this beast has been a lot of fun, but the bus does get only 5 or 6 miles to the gallon.

How does Wendy keep her weight down?

Losing weight is a trial when you are having a baby and nursing every year! I struggled for many years before I found "the key" for me. I decided one day that I was going to find out why I was overweight. I went and bought a new notebook and started writing down everything I put in my mouth, even a mint. I simply ate like I always did for about a week and found that I was eating way too many calories. Then I analyzed my log and thought of ways I could cut back on my unhealthy habits.

The result? I lost 40 pounds! That was 4 years ago and I have had three more kids since. I made it a regular habit to write down everything I ate, analyze the list, and figure out where I could feasibly cut back.

I also learned to exercise more. I really didn't exercise much other than chase kids and keep the house clean. I would consistently remind myself that I didn't need to be sitting around long. When I would feel the temptation to sit around, I would tell myself, "Wendy, get up and move!" So my motto to lose weight is, "Eat less; Move more!" Even bouncing your foot when you have to sit is burning calories. I came up with this plan out of necessity: I knew I couldn't join a fitness center or Weight Watchers.

Another important thing about my weight loss was being relaxed, not desperate, about it. I did stick to the real foods, real butter, real cream, eggs. I didn't just eat egg whites but the whole egg. I didn't buy any diet food. I read all the labels. I bought a food book that showed calories. I cut out white flour and white sugar as much as I could. Another trick I found was to try to eat every two hours even if it was just three bites of an apple or a few crackers.

I would not stuff myself at mealtime and would look forward to a little snack later. In the morning, as soon as my eyes open, I would take three bites of something to break the fast of overnight. When you starve yourself your body just goes into starvation mode and hangs onto everything, so you don't really lose weight. If you put three bites of something into your tummy every couple hours, you end up eating small meals and your body can "trust" you and will drop the weight. I saved desserts for special occasions and would be right back at it the next day. Sure, I had some days that I would overeat, but the key was to get back at it the next day. Have more good days than bad. Drink your eight or so glasses of good water every day. Soup is huge. A cup of soup is very satisfying but doesn't stuff you.

I figured that my stomach was a muscle and that I needed to shrink it. I was used to eating too much at once. I didn't think anything of thirds at dinnertime! Now I am content with a simple serving at mealtime and small healthy snacks throughout the day.

I had to watch out for false guilt. I hated to see things get thrown out, and I used to often finish my children's meals after dinner. I prayed and asked God to help me not to feel responsible for every scrap. He always met me there! So I stopped finishing any of the kids' plates or anything else.

The transformation has been so dramatic that some of my friends have asked me what happened to my face! My brother saw me after three years and he said I was 1/2 the size I used to be. I lost 10 sizes.

How do parents of so many kids find time for themselves?

We must be good at this, because we keep having kids! We go out on dates about every-other week. We roll a shopping trip into a quick meal, and we call it a date. Having teenagers at home able to watch the kids makes this possible. We pity the parents with very small children; finding a good babysitter is something we haven't had to wrestle with for many years.

About once every-other year we "get away" to Estes Park for a rendezvous. This last year some friends offered us their log cabin in the winter to enjoy. It was a great blessing!

How do you find enough time for each child?

This is a great question! It is usually asked by parents who spend a good deal of time with their one or two children, then do the math and find out they need 25 hours in a day to fit it in for a family our size. "It is impossible," they reason, "so a family of 13 kids must be more neglected than a small family."

Large families know that this isn't the case. One reason is because the strength of siblings is vital. The kids help each other and develop sibling relationships that, amazingly, substitute for the need for parents to fill that relational need. We try to find time for all our kids and work hard to accommodate, but we often will group them together. The older kids often stay up later than the little ones to enjoy one another or have the deeper conversations that they require.

Other ideas that allow us to find time for each child:

- Chris takes one kid to work one per week. It takes nearly three months to work through all the kids, but the time is rich.
- I (Wendy), when having to run to the store for something, will take one child. This gives me the time to talk individually with him or her.
- When a child brings me a cup of coffee in the morning, I take the time to talk with them.
- I give the child one-on-one time in our daily school.
- We pray corporately at night before sending the kids to bed, but I (Wendy) tuck the kids in bed individually.

What do you do for a living?

I (Chris) own three businesses, one of which is a nonprofit ministry. Between the three businesses, we bring home about $40,000 per year. This is enough for us to live comfortably and contently. I love the work that I do and, when I can, I incorporate the kids in the hustle bustle of it all. Here are explanations of each business:

1. Training Minds Ministry, an educational nonprofit 501c3 organization registered with the IRS, hosts academic debate camps across the nation. Based off 1 Peter 1:13 "Train the mind for action," the ministry's purpose is to train young people how to think, speak and persuade (in that order). See www.trainingminds.org.

2. Monument Publishing is the publishing firm for the ministry (and also the taxable side of the work we do). We publish curriculum, textbooks, handbooks, DVDs and CDs, study helps, and other resources that help prepare the student to compete in academic debate. See www.monumentpublishing.com.

3. Internet Asset Management & Consulting is my Internet development firm. I have my MBA with an emphasis in Electronic Business. My firm specializes in building websites, online applications, electronic marketing campaigns, and personal and business strategies. Though we specialize in Internet development, we like to say we're not as much in the Internet development business as we are in the "business development business." We build online business solutions that

run alongside already-existing offline businesses. I have two developers who help me take care of my clients. See www.internetassetmanager.com.

How did you write this book?

Wendy gave me a Christmas gift in 2005 of a written book on how to parent a dozen children. She got together in secret with a friend of hers and wrote a number of pages on the topic. The plan was to give the book to me so I could edit it and publish it.

It took nearly two years to get this done, but the TLC experience pushed the process along. I took on much of the work in the evenings at the office while Wendy cared for the kids. Wendy concluded with finishing touches and edits. The final result is the book you are finishing now.

Endnotes

[1] Hebrews 12:1-3. "Therefore, since we are surrounded by such a great cloud of witnesses, let us throw off everything that hinders and the sin that so easily entangles, and let us run with perseverance the race marked out for us. Let us fix our eyes on Jesus, the author and perfecter of our faith, who for the joy set before him endured the cross, scorning its shame, and sat down at the right hand of the throne of God. Consider him who endured such opposition from sinful men, so that you will not grow weary and lose heart."

[2] Joyce, Kathryn. "Arrows for the War," *The Nation.* November 27, 2006.

[3] Longman, Phillip. "The Return of Patriarchy." *Foreign Policy*, March/April 2006.

[4] Randall, Colin. "Middle-class French mothers will be paid to start le baby boom." *Telegraph.co.uk.* September 20, 2005.

[5] Philippians 4:6. "Be anxious for nothing, but in everything by prayer and supplication with thanksgiving let your requests be made known to God."

[6] There is no shortage of verses that speak of being "fruitful" and "increasing in number," all of which procreation is seen as a positive thing. See Gen. 1:22, 1:28, 8:17, 9:1, 9:7, 17:20, 35:11, 47:27, 48:4, Ex. 1:7, Lev. 26:9, Ps. 105:24, Jer. 23:3, and Ez. 36:11.

[7] Jesus referenced clothes several times in Matthew 6 as items *not to worry about* (Mt. 6:25, 28, 31 and 34).

[8] Early in our marriage when Chris was getting his undergraduate degree and Wendy was working fulltime, we took advantage of WIC. We got off WIC when Chris graduated and attained regular employment. That was the last time we were on government assistance. We have always seen government assistance as exactly that (*assistance*) and we try to stay off it as much as possible.

---

[9] Galatians 5:1. The value of freedom appears throughout the New Testament, but modern sermons frequently center on heaven and hell, salvation, end-times, prophesy, and many other popular topics. While these topics are important to Christians, we believe the topic of freedom isn't given fair airtime. This is a subject that intrigues many non-Christians and is likely one of the most persuasive topics for conversions.

[10] It goes without reason that most anti-spanking activists aren't parents themselves. They are typically folks who had poor experiences with abuse when they were children. Abuse is definitely a concern, but allowing a child to be unbuckled in a van is also disturbing. These folks are usually at a loss when met with such a conflict, but parents are dealt these conflicts all the time when raising children.

[11] Kluger, Jeffrey. "How your siblings make you who you are." *TIME*. July 10, 2006.

[12] To help set the record straight, we had Alicia approve these final chapters. She has been an active participant in the discussion of love and how important it is for families to discuss these matters. Lest you think we are revealing private details of her life, rest assured that Alicia agrees and approves.

[13] We grew to trust the onsite producer very much, but editors we never met were going to assemble the finished product slated to air on TLC. Hats off to everyone involved in this project, for all of us (including Alicia) believe that what was presented was reasonably fair and accurate. It wasn't pretty—there were things said on the show that captured the difficult reality of the situation—but none of us feel the footage was taken out of context or was a manipulation of the truth.